GW01374687

ALFA ROMEO SPIDER
1955-86

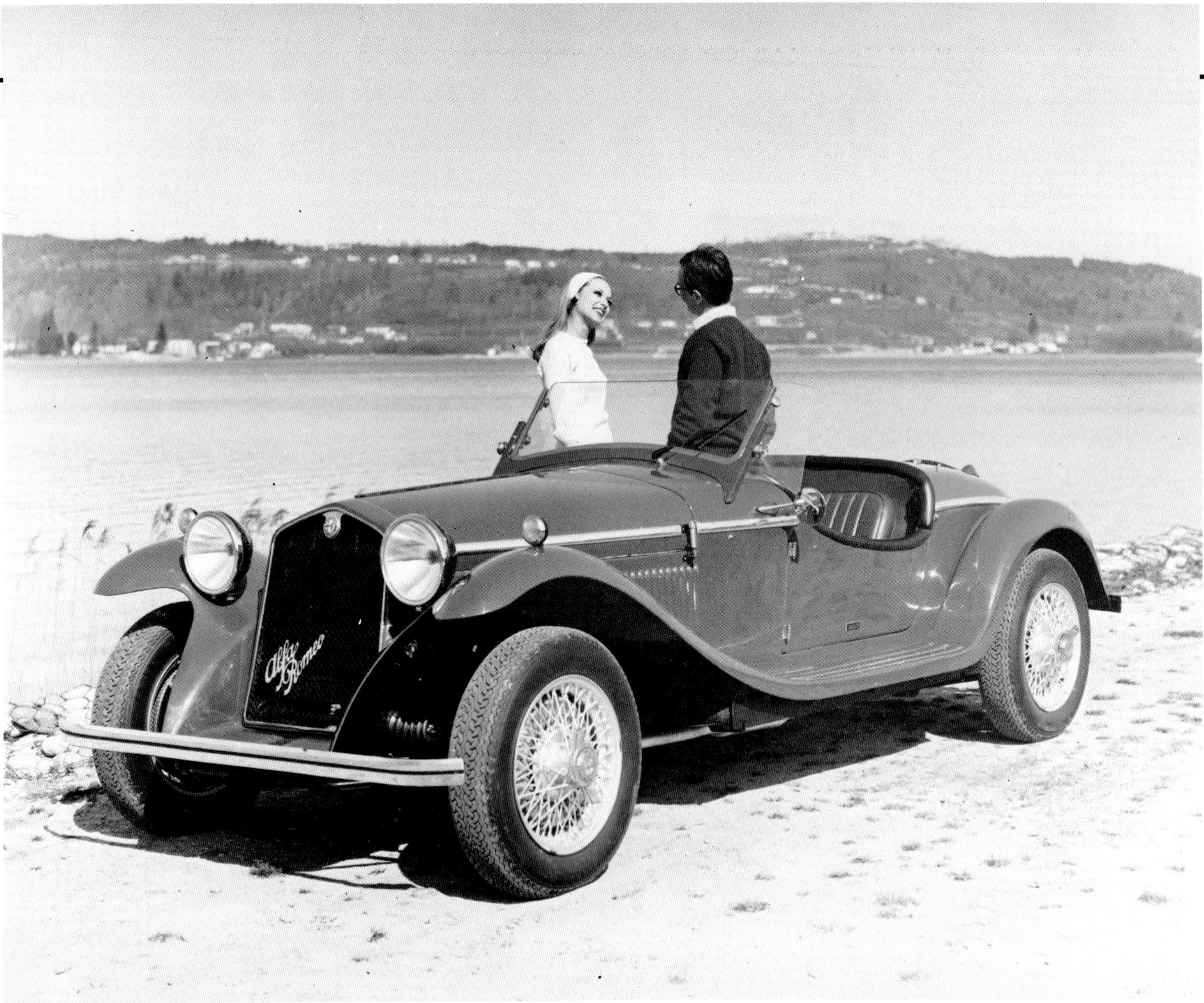
Alfa Romeo

ALFA ROMEO SPIDER

1955-86

A Documentation by Walter Zeichner

Schiffer Publishing Ltd

1469 Morstein Road, West Chester, Pennsylvania 19380

This volume of the Schiffer Automotive Series is devoted to the Alfa Romeo convertibles that, under the name of "Spider", have won great numbers of admirers all over the world since the appearance of the famous Giulietta. We have tried to bring together the important advertising material from various eras and obtain authentic factory photos in order to show the vehicles as they left the assembly line. With few exceptions, all Spider bodywork was made by either Pininfarina or Touring, and we are indebted to these firms for their documentary materials. The firm of Alfa Romeo in Arese and their German representatives in Frankfurt am Main have also contributed to our materials. In addition, the assistance of Messrs. Georg Amtmann, Robert Horender, Kai Jacobsen and Jan Norbye has also enriched this volume. As an illustrated book of automobile nostalgia, this volume of the Schiffer Automotive Series will surely awaken memories of the Fifties among the older generation—in those days one bought an Alfa from an NSU dealer!—or inspire dreams among the younger automobile fans, to whom a Spider from Italy is an undying classic, a timeless piece of perfect technology that can still be bought. Still—for how long there will still be an Alfa Romeo Spider, no one can say.

Halwart Schrader
Editor

Translated from the German by Dr. Edward Force.

Copyright © 1989 by Schiffer Publishing Ltd..
Library of Congress Catalog Number: 89-084167.

All rights reserved. No part of this work may be reproduced or used in any forms or by any means—graphic, electronic or mechanical, including photocopying or information storage and retrieval systems—without written permission from the copyright holder.

Printed in the United States of America.
ISBN: 0-88740-195-3
Published by Schiffer Publishing Ltd.
1469 Morstein Road, West Chester, Pennsylvania 19380

Originally published under the title "Alfa Romeo Spider" 1955-86, Schrader Motor Chronik, copyright Schrader Automobil-Bücher, Handels-GmbH, München, West Germany, © 1986, ISBN: 3-922617-13-1.

Please write for a free catalog.
This book may be purchased from the publisher.
Please include $2.00 postage.
Try your bookstore first.

Contents

The photo on page two shows a Quattro-route Zagato, built from 1966 to 1968.

Above: Alfa Romeo 2600 Spider, introduced in the spring of 1962, body by Touring Milano.

The Spider Story: 1955-86	6
Lively Speedster: Giulietta Spider	10
A New Four—Cylinder: Alfa Spider 2000	15
The Alfa Romeo 2600	19
Giulia 1600 Spider	21
Giulia Sprint GTC	32
1750 Spider Veloce	33
1300 Junior Spider	35
2000 Spider Veloce	41
The 1600 Renaissance	48
Technical Data: Alfa Romeo Spider 1955—86	82
Alfa Romeo Spider in the Press	84
Alfa Romeo Spider in Miniature	90
Literature for Alfa Romeo Fans	94
Alfa Romeo Clubs	95

The Spider Story: 1955-86

"Whoever loves having the wind blowing past his nose, whoever enjoys physically feeling the fast movement of his car, for him this car is the fulfillment of his dreams."

This sentence comes from a brochure for the Alfa Romeo Giulietta Spider at the end of the Fifties. It expresses in vivid words what the fascination of the open sports car means to the tradition-rich Milan automobile manufacturer. The Giulietta Spider was the first in a long line of two-seaters that extends into our own day to offer the lover of thoroughbred cars a car that, when handled right, guaranteed the highest degree of driving pleasure combined with a classically beautiful form.

The ancestor of the Giulietta coupes and sedans, and thus also of the Spiders developed from them, was the Type 1900, which came on the market in 1950 and introduced a new era in the Alfa Romeo firm, the beginning of large-series automobile production. Until then the firm's main activities had been auto racing and the production of expensive luxury cars with 2.5-liter engines, which were made and sold in small numbers. This policy, frankly, had not helped to improve the shaky financial situation of the firm, which also had to recover from heavy war damage. Only the good sales of the new middle-class 1900 car brought relief and paved the way to the development of an even smaller and lower-priced

Left: Earliest ancestor of all Alfa Spiders, the 24 HP sports car of 1910—that was the year the firm was founded.

Above: One of the most famous sports cars from the Alfa Romeo firm was the 6C1750. Here is a 1929 Super Sport.

model with a 1300-cc motor. The Giulietta made her debut in 1954 as a coupe, and in the summer of the following year (what season could have been more suited to the introduction of a Spider?) the open two-seater version was introduced.

The powerplant for the Giulietta series had been derived from the 1900 motor developed by Chief Engineer Dr. Puliga, an engine that differed from most middle-class engines in its expensive means of construction. This powerplant, expressly designed for sport, featured dual overhead camshafts which activated the valves directly and made the motor's high running speed possible. The engine block and cylinder head were made of light metal, the crankshaft had five bearings, the pistons moved in cylinder units surrounded by cool water, enabling worn parts to be replaced easily. This low-vibration and silky-soft motor was installed in all Giulietta models and originally developed 80 HP in the Spider version, which sufficed for a top speed of over 150 kph. The excitingly beautiful bodywork was a design from the house of Pininfarina, as were those of most Spiders in future series, while Bertone was always responsible for the design of the coupes. The whole technology originated with this coupe version, known as the Sprint, and was embodied in the shortened Spider chassis.

Two persons sat comfortably in the Alfa Romeo Giulietta Spider and could make use of luggage space that was quite respectable for that class of car, since the spare wheel was stored behind the seats. There the no-frills top, typical of the Spider, could be stowed, ready to be raised easily for a sudden shower and also capable of protecting the occupants dependably from the influences of rough weather. When the cold season came, one could turn the Spider into a closed car with a hardtop that blended harmoniously with the body lines. For particularly zealous sports-car enthusiasts who thirsted for high performance, Alfa Romeo marketed a more powerful

Left: One of the few Spiders that was bodied by Bertone—a prototype based on the Giulietta, built in 1955.

version in 1956, the Spider Veloce, with engine compression of 9.1:1 instead of 8.5:1, and with two double-throat carburetors richly supplying it with fuel, so that 90 HP were available to move the little speedster at almost 180 kph. As beautiful and perfect as these machines were, they had one notable weak point: a high degree of stress right after starting in low temperatures, which rarely bothered them in sunny Italy, but in Germany and elsewhere, alas, could greatly reduce the fun of driving a car almost half the year. Whoever did not let his Alfa work its way up to operating temperature for a time at moderate engine speed before starting to go fast soon had to expect motor damage, which contributed to the car's acquiring a certain reputation for trouble. Otherwise these machines, as well as all the later versions with higher engine displacements, are fine models of cultivation, that bore even hard use without complaint and could achieve above-average performance. When the Giulia sedan appeared in July of 1962, the Spider soon was adapted to this larger machine. In 1964 the hottest Spider version to that time, the 1600 Veloce, was introduced, with the same engine displacement (but 9.7:1 compression) now able to produce a respectable 112 HP instead of only 92, making the car capable of almost 190 kph and standing out particularly by its quick acceleration. In form, the 1600 Spider differed from its somewhat less powerful but no less charming predecessors only in having a wider air-scoop on the hood. The strong Spider had also gained a new name, since Giulietta (Juliet in English) probably no longer seemed appropriate for such a potent car; thus the new Spider was called Giulia along with the strangely styled sedan.

Production Spider of 1962, bodied by Pininfarina, today a desirable collector car, although not exactly an oldtimer.

These small Spiders were not all that Alfa Romeo had to offer open sports-car fans in the late Fifties and early Sixties. In 1958 the 1900, by now rather long in the tooth, was replaced by a big, powerful sedan with a 2-liter dual overhead camshaft motor, and had Touring design a suitable Spider version. This 2000 Spider was very reminiscent of the Pininfarina Spider in terms of styling, but was longer and wider and appeared more low-slung. The splendid 2-liter engine had relatively low compression at 8.5:1 and featured great flexibility and tremendous passing power. This machine developed 115 HP and let the beautiful car reach a top speed of 175 kph. The 2000 Spider was also rather more comfortable than the small spider, which could be described as a man's sports car; it was often and happily driven by women.

The sales figures for this medium-sized sports car naturally fell well behind those of the Giulietta and Giulia, since the price of 2.5 million Lire was considerably higher than those of its smaller relatives. As early as 1961 the production of this type ended at 3443 examples, and it ranks as one of the rarities from the house of Alfa Romeo today.

But there was another increase. At the Geneva Auto Show in 1962 the Milan firm presented its new upper-class 2600 model series, consisting of Berlina, Sprint and Spider, all powered by a new 6-cylinder motor with Alfa's typical dual overhead camshafts, seven-bearing crankshaft and, in its most powerful version, with three double carburetors, developing 145 HP with a 9:1 compression ratio, and thus assuring that the 2+2 version with body by Touring could reach a speed of 200 kph. But the most impressive feature was the way this power increased with a soft touch, while the precise and easy-shifting five-speed gearbox was a joy to use. Naturally, such exclusive features had their price, adding up to almost 3 million Lire, though this did not keep true lovers away. Exactly 2255 Spider versions were produced through 1965, the first 1310 of which still had rear drum brakes. Meanwhile it had to be recognized that the beloved Giulia Spider was also getting old despite its supposedly timeless, exciting styling, and this led to the development of a new small open sports car, which meant in this case that pininfarina created a new dress for proven technology. This somewhat individualistic but no less characteristic bodywork was, incidentally, the last design from the hand of the firm's founder, Battista Pininfarina.

The famous designer obviously placed great emphasis on rounded forms in dressing this 1600 Spider, as it bore no similarity to its ancestor. The long rounded rear and the main headlights, covered with aerodynamic plexiglas covers, were particularly eye-catching. The whole car had become significantly longer, wider and somewhat lower, and thanks to its clear and elegantly simple styling without superficial effects, it was truly destined to correspond to public taste for a long time. In Italy the new car was popularly known as "Osso di sepia", in reference to the similarity of its longish body to the oval remains of octopi found on many Italian beaches. Alfa Romeo itself had a hard time finding a new name for the 1600 Spider, and so a competition was announced to find the nicest name.

In the end the name "Duetto" won. It was first introduced as a new name for the Spider, but the fans didn't like that at all, and soon the open sports cars were again called simply "Spider". Outstanding test results of the new 1600 cars were made public, and with a price of 12,990 Marks it was a good buy in Germany too. Before this type was replaced, in the very next year, by the more powerful 1750 cc version, 6325 of them had been built.

In the same year as the Duetto was born, a nostalgic car appeared under the Alfa Romeo name, the Spider 4 R Zagato, of which 92 were sold between 1966 and 1968. This car, largely unknown today, was a nice replica of the legendary Type 1750 of the Thirties, and had been inspired by the Italian automobile magazine *Quattroruote*.

The Spider 1750 Veloce, introduced in 1967, had 200 cc and 9 HP more to offer than the 1600 version, giving the engine, which was scarcely to be improved upon, a top speed of over 190 kph and needed scarcely ten seconds to accelerate from a standing start to 100 kph.

In 1970 the Spider's rounded tail was cut off, which pleased many customers and created the lines that are still in style today. In addition, the dashboard

1955-56   Lively Speedster: Giulietta Spider

was redesigned to look completely different, a dual-circuit braking system and hanging foot pedals were introduced, the seats were improved and several other minor cosmetic changes were made.

Two years before, the beginner's model for Spider fans was introduced at the Geneva Auto Show: the 1300 Junior, which still reached a top speed of over 170 kph with its 89 HP but cost almost a quarter less than the 1750 Veloce. In June of 1971 the long-lived Spider 2000 Veloce finally appeared, with its engine displacing 2 liters thanks to a bore increase of 4 mm.

After only six years, more than 20,000 cars of this type had been sold, and with minor changes (including thick rubber front and rear coverings), such a classic Italian Spider can still be obtained—and enjoyed—today!

The first Spider appeared in 1955 as a convertible variant of the Giulietta Coupe. Series production began in 1956. The car, with body by Pininfarina, made many friends from the start—there were delivery delays of up to six months, as Pininfarina did not then deign to build more than 1000 of them within twelve months. For the sake of historical accuracy, the Turin coachbuilding firm's name was then written in two words: Pinin Farina.

Luggage compartment

The luggage compartment of Giulietta spider offers a big, free space and an easily, proper arrangement of the luggage.

The three instruments can be read at a glance because they are grouped on a suitable panel of modern design. Bearing in mind the sport features of the car, there is also a revolution counter. On the instrument panel we find also the control switch for ventilation and anti-freezing. Provision for a radio receiver is made in the center of the fascia plate, but it is not included in the normal outfit of the car. The upper part of the instrument panel is screened, so as to avoid any disturbances by reflection; for the same reason the steering wheel is black. The gear box shift is by center lever.

Above and right: Brochure for the 1957 Giulietta. It is an English edition—efforts to market the car in the USA were highly stressed!

Transformability

The Giulietta spider, when closed, has all the technical features of a practical drophead: the side windows lowerable with a crankhandle, fit in the windscreen with perfect tightness. The opening of the hood is extremely easy. It reenters into its post on the rear of the seats, where are also placed a spare tire and tools. When opened, the car is perfectly shaped with the only projection of the wind-screen.

Left: This is how the first advertising material for the new Spider looked in 1955-57—really quite undramatic in view of the excitingly lovely car.

11

1959

Left: Title page of a 1959 Giulietta brochure, not a reprint of an Italian original, but produced by NSU.

Below: The Spider had a stick shift, the Berlina (sedan) had its shift on the steering column. The Farina firm's trademark was an internationally recognized sign of quality for the body.

Giulietta Spider - der Wagen für junge Herzen!

Wer es liebt, sich den Wind um die Nase wehen zu lassen, wer Freude daran hat, die schnelle Fahrt seines Wagens körperlich zu spüren, dem ist dieses Auto die Erfüllung seiner Träume. Es gibt einfach keinen reineren Fahrgenuss als den in diesem spritzigen Cabriolet. Solch ein Traumauto kann natürlich nicht »billig« sein. Wie jeder Alfa Romeo, wird auch der Spider nicht in Großserie auf den Markt gebracht - jedes Stück ist individuell gearbeitet und mit Liebe vollendet.

Deshalb auch haftet diesem Fahrzeug der Hauch des Besonderen, des Persönlichen an. Und doch kann man den Alfa Romeo guten Gewissens preiswert nennen - gemessen an dem, was er seinem Besitzer bietet. Er hat Charakter, dieser Wagen! Und die Mitwelt bleibt betrachtend stehen, wo immer er als Star zwischen den Autos des Alltags auftaucht. Pinin Farina schuf das Kleid für dieses Sportcabriolet. Sein Zeichen - rechts abgebildet und jedem Spider aufgeprägt - gilt in aller Welt als Bürgschaft für höchste Leistung in Form und Stil.

Hinter dem Volant

Der Spider ist ein zweisitziges Cabriolet. Die breitflächige Panoramascheibe schützt Fahrer und Beifahrer vor dem anbrausenden Fahrtwind, und doch bekommen Sie soviel Luft und Sonnenschein herein, wie Sie sich nur wünschen. Bei aller Sportlichkeit fährt sich's dank der körpergerechten Schalensessel in diesem Wagen ausgesprochen gemütlich. Ein elegantes Fahrzeug für glückliche Reisen zu zweit!

Giulietta Spider—the car for young hearts!

Whoever loves to feel the wind blow over his nose, whoever enjoys the physical feel of a fast-moving car, for him this car is a dream come true. There is simply no purer joy in driving than that of a lively convertible. Such a dream car naturally cannot be "cheap". Like every Alfa Romeo, the Spider is not put on the market in large series—every one is built individually and finished with love.

That is why the aura of the special, the personal surrounds this car. And yet one can call the Alfa Romeo reasonably priced with a clear conscience—in terms of what it offers its owner. It has character, this car! And the world stops and watches wherever it appears like a star among everyday cars. Pinin Farina created the dress for this sports roadster. His emblem—shown at right and found on every Spider—is known all over the world as a guarantee of the highest achievement in form and style.

Behind the wheel

The Spider is a two-seat convertible. The wide panoramic windshield protects the driver and passenger from the vigorous airstream, and yet you get so much fresh air and sunshine inside as you could want. With all its sportiness, a ride in this car is particularly comfortable thanks to the bucket seats built to fit the human body. An elegant car for happy driving for two!

Wie man sich bettet, so fährt man, - könnte man hier sagen. Die Abbildung links zeigt, dass Spider-Fahrer es in dieser Hinsicht gut haben. Selbstverständlich sind die beiden komfortablen Schalensessel einzeln verschiebbar. Kleine Seitenscheiben sorgen dafür, dass es auch bei offenem Verdeck nicht ungebührlich zieht. ● Ein wassergekühlter Vierzylinder-Motor mit zwei obenliegenden Nockenwellen ist für Wagen vom Charakter der Giulietta-Reihe genau das Richtige. Wie er beim Spider in sein Gehäuse eingepasst ist, zeigt das Bild links unten. ● Wurde im Motorraum mit Platz tunlichst gespart, so ist der Kofferraum im Heck grosszügig bemessen. Das Reserverad wurde im toten Raum hinter den Sitzlehnen verstaut. So ist der Kofferraum glattflächig, übersichtlich und ohne Verwinkelung, ein Merkmal, das die Fahrer freut, ebenso wie die Tatsache, dass der Kofferraumdeckel weit zu öffnen ist, wodurch das Ein- und Ausladen des Gepäcks erleichtert wird.

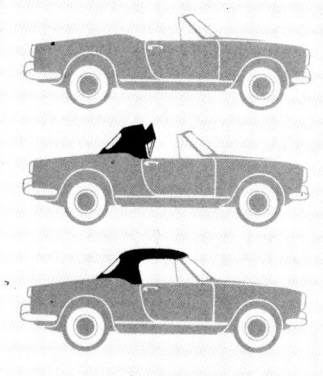

Island-Tiefs und Wetterfronten aus Skandinavien sind für den Spider-Fahrer ohne Schrecken: Mit wenigen Griffen das Faltverdeck vorgezogen und gespannt, die Seitenfenster hochgekurbelt - schon sitzt man unter Dach und Fach. Dass die klassische Linie und die sportliche Form des Wagens darunter nicht leiden, dafür hat Meister Farina natürlich gesorgt.

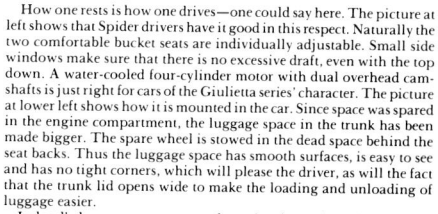

How one rests is how one drives—one could say here. The picture at left shows that Spider drivers have it good in this respect. Naturally the two comfortable bucket seats are individually adjustable. Small side windows make sure that there is no excessive draft, even with the top down. A water-cooled four-cylinder motor with dual overhead camshafts is just right for cars of the Giulietta series' character. The picture at lower left shows how it is mounted in the car. Since space was spared in the engine compartment, the luggage space in the trunk has been made bigger. The spare wheel is stowed in the dead space behind the seat backs. Thus the luggage space has smooth surfaces, is easy to see and has no tight corners, which will please the driver, as will the fact that the trunk lid opens wide to make the loading and unloading of luggage easier.

Iceland's low-pressure areas and weather fronts from Scandinavia are no problem for the Spider driver: with a few moves the folded top is raised and spread, the side windows rolled up—and one sits snugly under the roof. Master Farina naturally made sure that the classic lines and sporting form of the car are not detracted from by it.

t für Alltagsmenschen

esen Seiten möchten wir Ihnen die Alfa Romeo-Automobile vorstellen, jene Wagen, die mit besten der Welt gehören. Die Alfa Romeos werden nicht in Großserie hergestellt und man ie nicht an jeder Strassenecke. Ihre Fahrer sind keine Alltagsmenschen, und nur derjenige den Wert und die Rasse eines Alfa Romeo zu schätzen, der sich ein junges Herz bewahrt hat den das Fahren mehr darstellt als nur ein Transport von A-Dorf nach B-Stadt. Dem Durchsbürger steht ein Durchschnittswagen gewiss gut zu Gesicht. Menschen von besonderem aber wünschen Wagen von besonderem Format.

vom Format des Alfa Romeo. Rassig, schön und temperamentvoll - so präsentiert sich dieser aliener als Nonplusultra des Autobaus. Einen Alfa Romeo fahren heisst, die ausgetretenen er Alltäglichkeit verlassen. Und es heisst, das Fahrerlebnis in der Vollendung geniessen. er nicht etwa in einem Strassenkreuzer von gewaltigen Dimensionen oder in einem hochemhen Pistenrenner! Der Alfa Romeo ist vielmehr ein handlicher, spritziger, sportlicher Tourender sich mit spielerischer Leichtigkeit lenken lässt, - ein Wagen, der so recht zu Menschen it jungem Herzen.

sst, Alfa Romeo bringt natürlich nicht nur einen einzigen Typ auf den deutschen Markt. Unter esievollen Namen «Giulietta» präsentiert sich eine Reihe von sechs verschiedenen Modellen. ta Sprint» nennt sich das bildschöne, elegante 80-PS-Coupe, das wir links im Bild oben vormöchten. Mit etwas abgeändertem 90-PS-Motor heisst dieser Wagen «Giulietta Sprint Veloce». ers sportliche Fahrer werden sich für das in der Mitte abgebildete zweisitzige Cabriolet ieren. Mit dem 70-PS-Motor trägt es den schnellen Namen «Giulietta Spider», mit dem 90-PS-e den noch schnelleren Namen «Giulietta Spider Veloce». Bliebe das Fahrzeug unten: - bis Fünfsitzer für die Familie, in seiner sportlichen Konzeption ebenfalls ein Wagen mit rer Note. Als «Giulietta Berlina» bringt es 53 PS mit, als «Giulietta Berlina T.I.» leistet er 65 PS. t, ob Spider, ob Berlina - jeder Typ ein Wagen von unverwechselbarer Rasse,

jeder Typ ein echter *Alfa Romeo*

Above: The catalog text spoke of "Master Farina" in reference to the body design. In fact, the Spider looked equally good with its top up or down. A final word about this catalog: What comes from NSU is correct! The German-Italian cooperation worked well.

Left: Opening text in the catalog shown above and on the opposite page. Its simple words stressed the noble origins of the Alfa Romeo. An honest text that even includes useful technical data. One did not need to read about top speeds.

Not for everyday folks

In these pages we would like to introduce the Alfa Romeo automobiles to you, those cars that rank among the best in the world. The Alfa Romeos are not produced in large series, and one does not see them at every street corner. Their drivers are not everyday people, and only the person who has kept a young heart and regards driving as more than transport from A-ville to B-town knows how to appreciate the value and the breeding of an Alfa Romeo. A typical car will certainly suit the typical citizen. But people of a special type want a special type of car.

A car like the Alfa Romeo. A thoroughbred, beautiful and spirited—this true Italian car presents itself as the Non-plus-ultra of car building. Driving an Alfa Romeo means leaving the well-worn paths of everyday life. And it means enjoying the experience of driving to the fullest. But not in a turnpike cruiser of mighty dimensions or a highly sensitive racer! The Alfa Romeo is rather a handy, peppy, sporty touring car that handles with playful lightness—a car that fits people with young hearts just right.

That means Alfa Romeo naturally does not put just one type on the German market. Under the poetic name of "Giulietta" are a series of six different models. "Giulietta Sprint" is the beautiful, elegant 80-HP coupe shown at left above. With a somewhat modified 90-HP motor this car is called "Giulietta Sprint Veloce". Particularly sporting drivers will be interested in the two-seater convertible depicted in the center. With its 70-HP motor is bears the lively name of "Giulietta Spider", with the 90-HP engine, the even faster name of "Giulietta Spider Veloce". There remains the car shown below, a four- to five-seater for the family, in terms of its sporting design likewise a car with a special spirit. As the "Giulietta Berlina" it produces 65 HP. Whether Sprint, Spider or Berlina—every type is a car of unmistakable breeding.

Every type a genuine **Alfa Romeo**.

13

Technical Data

	Giulietta **Sprint** Coupe	Giulietta **Sprint Veloce** Coupe	Giulietta **Spider** Convertible	Giulietta **Spider Veloce** Convertible	Giulietta **Berlina T. I.** Sport Sedan
Horsepower	80	90	80	90	65
Top speed (kph)	170	180	160	175	155
Fuel consumption (liters/100km)	9	11	9	11	8.5
Carburetor	Solex downdraft 2-stage	Weber double-throat, oil cooler	Solex downdraft 2-stage	Weber double-throat, oil cooler	Solex downdraft 2-stage
Gearshift	←——— central stick shift ———→				Steering column shift
Speeds in gears (kph)					
First	51	54	48	54	42
Second	89	92	82	92	72
Third	125	133	118	133	107
Fourth	170	180	155	175	155
Chassis					
Wheelbase (mm)	2380	2380	2200	2200	2380
Fuel capacity (liters)	53	80	53	80	42
Dimensions					
Length (mm)	3980	3980	3860	3860	3990
Width (mm)	1535	1535	1580	1580	1558
Height (mm)	1320	1320	1250/1335	1250/1335	1407
Turning circle	11	11	9.6	9.6	11
Weight (kg)	850	780	820	830	880
Body type	Coupe 2+2	Coupe 2+2	Open two-seater	Open two-seater	4-door Sedan

Motor: 1290-cc four-cylinder with dual overhead camshafts; water-cooled; bore 74mm, stroke 75 mm, light-metal cylinder heads, pressure lubrication; oil filter; 12-volt electric system.

Transmission: Four-speed gearbox, fully synchronized; single-plate dry clutch.

Chassis: Self-supporting body; wheel suspension and springs; two triangular front links, coil springs, shock absorbers and transverse stabilizer, rigid rear axle with triangular links for transverse action and two longitudinal links, coil springs and shock absorbers; tire size 155-15"; hydraulic foot brakes, front Duplex, rear Simplex, light-metal drums with cast rings and cooling fins with fan effect; front track 1286 mm, rear track 1270 mm.

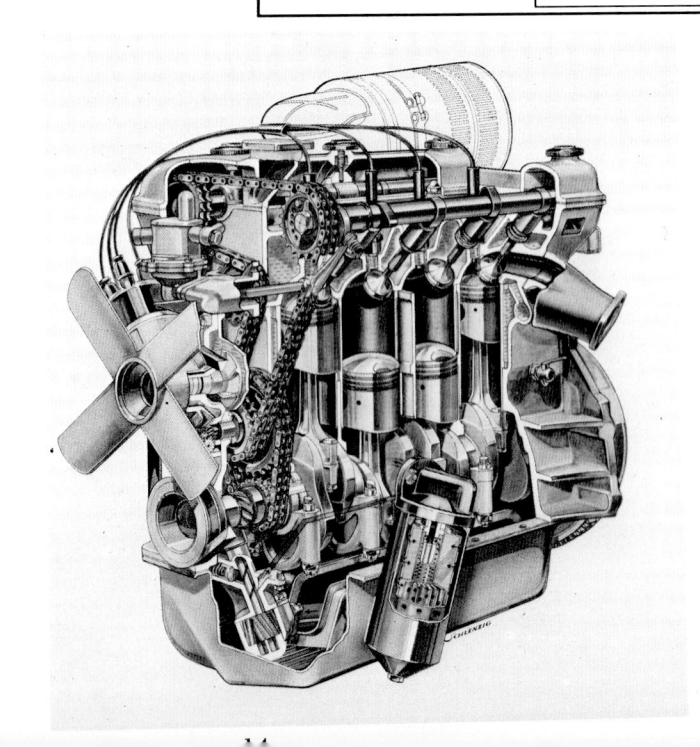

Naturally one could easily get the spirited dual overhead camshaft powerplant to use more than 11 liters in 100 kilometers if one drove a sporting car like the Alfa Romeo in a sporting manner. And here they are at last, the top speeds: the Spider Veloce reached 175 kph. In 1959 that was unusually fast ...

A big new four-cylinder: Alfa 2000

In 1958 Alfa Romeo presented the 2000, which could also be had as a Spider. The elegant long and lightly built body came from Touring of Milan ("Superleggera"), a firm with a long tradition and decades of association with the house of Alfa.

Title page of the first catalog for the 2000 Spider. A completely new image of graphic design, that was not used very often.

15

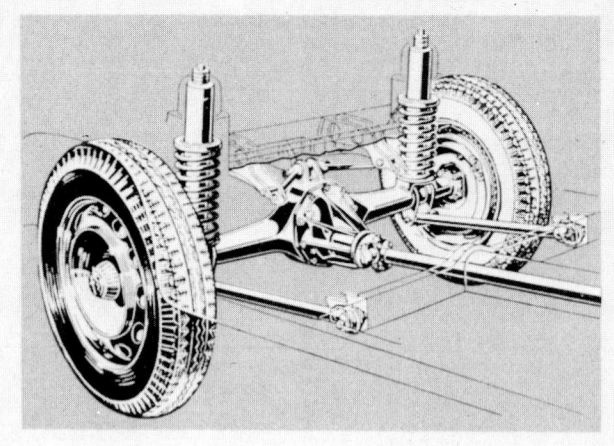

technical features

Number of cylinders		4
Bore and stroke	mm	84.5 × 88
Piston displacement	cc	1975
Horsepower	HP 115	(HP-SAE 133)
Maximum revolutions	r.p.m.	5700
Front track		4' 7"
Rear track		4' 6"
Wheel base		8' 2"
Minimum turning circle		15' 9"
Overall length		14' 4"
Overall width		5' 5"
Overall height		2' 11"
Dry weight	lbs	2649
Fuel consumption	m.p.g.	20
Maximum speed	m.p.h.	109
Seats		2
Tyre size		165 × 400
Electrical system		12 Volt - 50 Amp. Hrs.
Fuel tank	gals	15.8

The flexibility of the **suspension** in the « 2000 Spider » is superb. The rubber pads have a progressive action and keep the car on an even keel, even on the most difficult bends.

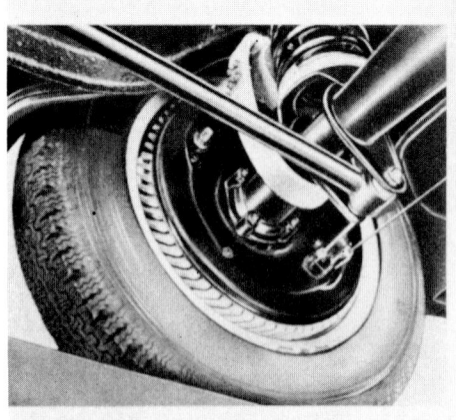

The **brake system** is typical Alfa Romeo; in front, the « 2000 Spider » has a two leading shoes brake type, while all the four drums are equipped with helicoidal fins for cooling.

Clutch: single dry-plate, hydraulically operated.

Valve gear: inclined valves in the hemispherical cylinder head, cams acting directly on valve stems, spring cap oil cups, double overhead camshafts.

Gear-box: 5 synchronized forward speeds and 1 reverse. Ball gear shift lever.

Front suspension: independent with transverse linkage, coil springs, stabilizing bar and telescopic hydraulic shock absorbers.
Rear suspension: rigid axle housing with upper triangular thrust rods and lower radius rods, coil springs, hydraulic and telescopic shock absorbers.

Differential: with hypoid bevel gears.

Left hand drive, by worm and roller.

Brakes: hydraulic, the front with two leading shoes; helical cooling fins on the drums.

The above data are only nominal

ALFA ROMEO S.P.A. · VIA GATTAMELATA, 45 · TELEFONO 39.77 · MILANO

D. C. Pro. 4 - 1959 (1) Printed in Italy - Istituto Grafico Bertieri - Milano

1958

Right: Inside the catalog for the 2000 shown on page 15.

Left: Native products were seldom presented to the Americans with as much technical detail.

18

The Alfa Romeo 2600

Geneva Salon 1962: Alfa Romeo presented its new model, the 2600, a "big" car that could be had in Spider form until 1965. 2255 of the chic cabriolets were made. This 200-kph car was seen as a cultivated and technically advanced automobile, thoroughly comparable with a Mercedes-Benz of the SL series.

Left: Two pictures from a catalog for the 2000 with body by Touring.

Right: Thus was the new 2600 presented: sprightly and happy . . .

Advertisements for the Giulietta Spider, which was still available along with the bigger models. The ladies appear a bit understated.

Aspetto frontale - La forma avvolgente del parabrezza con i montanti esternamente affusolati, la linea arditamente sfuggente del cofano, il pronunciato risalto dei doppi fari, la brillante soluzione della mascherina nella elegante calandra, il robusto paraurti avvolgente anche i fianchi, conferiscono al muso della 2600 spider una inconfondibile fisionomia altamente sportiva e signorile.

Aspetto posteriore - Le ardite pinne verticali, alloggianti tutti gli elementi di segnalazione formano, con il piano orizzontale del robusto paraurti, un tutt'uno squisitamente decorativo.

Baule - Di alta classe è l'armonia delle linee della coda, dove si apre un baule di grande capacità e di praticissimo accesso, reso ancora più funzionale dalla sistemazione della ruota di scorta sotto il piano di fondo.

The first color catalog for the 2600 Spider, which appeared in 1962, had a lively title page (page 19, above), but inside the mood was definitely factual. All pictures were studio photos, and the production of advertising material was now done in Italy.

Giulia 1600 Spider

1962 is the birth date of the new Spider 1600, once again a Pininfarina creation based on the Giulia—now a true large-series production car. In its first year of production alone, 3145 of the open cars were built, and 3875 in the next year. This car, later named the Duetto, was thus not an exclusive rarity like its forerunner. Yet one did not see the car on European roads very often, for the majority of the Spiders that were made were sold in the United States. Later there were body changes (round tail!), but not much changed in technical terms.

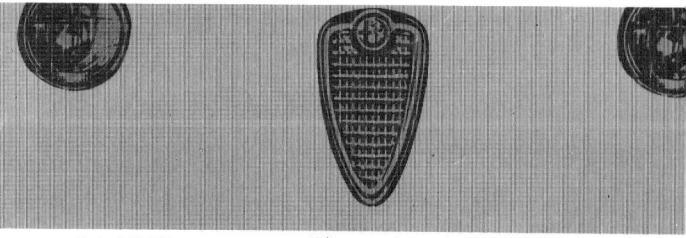

LA VOITURE QUI LIE À LA VÔTRE SA PERSONNALITÉ

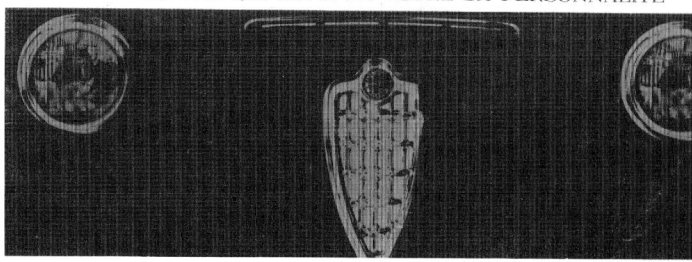

A very lavishly designed catalog for the new 1600 version. Separate covers of thin transparent material stressed the hardtop construction and provided graphic effects. This brochure was printed in six languages in 1963.

Right: Alfa Romeo came out with fully new advertising material in 1964. This is the title page of a brochure for the 1600 and 2600 sports cars.

Two more pages from the interesting catalog for the new Giulia 1600 of 1963. Headrests and seat belts were not yet mentioned then. But safety was made an important item, though the Alfa still did not have disc brakes.

1964

spider Alfa Romeo

1964

Lady with a big heart

The Giulia spider has confounded even the most experienced professional drivers with her ample generosity in pick-up, speed and roadability. Let's look inside the engine. Dual overhead camshafts, sodium-cooled valves, counter-balanced crankshaft with five main bearings and separately-ducted exhaust manifold. This power-plant enables the Giulia spider to reach speeds of over 105 mph. At 80 mph, it uses only half of its total power; an extraordinary reserve of power if needed. The 55 hp in reserve insures a lightning-like pick-up. This is an important reason why the engine will out-live and consume less gas than other engines exerting maximum horsepower to attain the same speed. Acceleration time from 0 to 60 mph is a mere 11.5 seconds; 0 to 80 mph, 19 seconds. The five forward speed gearbox is fully synchronized for driving under all road conditions. Fifth gear is extremely flexible and may be used through a wide range of speeds. The carburetor has two barrels with automatic control on the second. An accellerator pump allows for proper gas flow for instantaneous return to high rpm's. The assurance of instant accelleration response and quick maneuvering in congested traffic are inherent in the Giulia spider.

Giulia spider

1964

Left: A bird's-eye view of the 2600 Spider. With its wheelbase 25 cm longer (2500 instead of 2250 mm), this model could be made as a 2+2 that also had a large trunk.

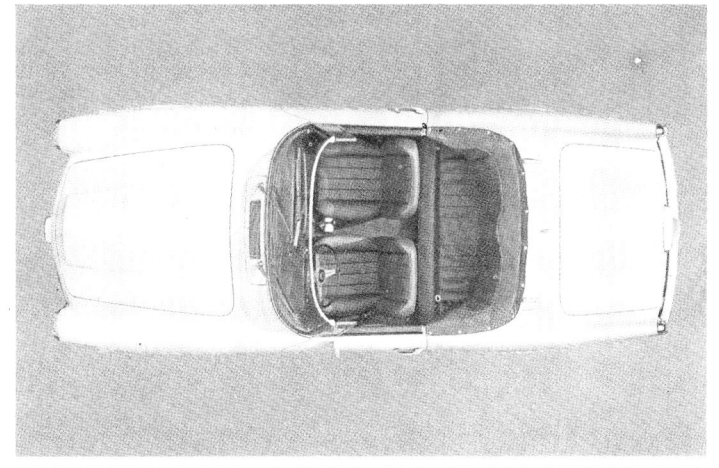

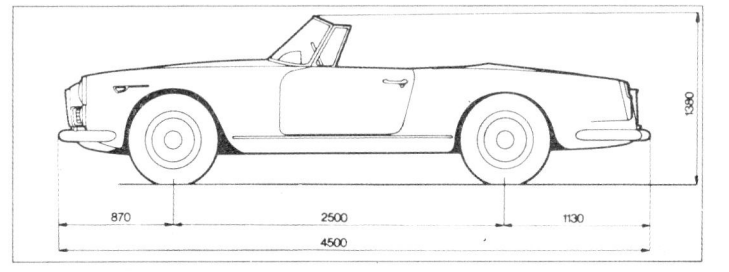

Left: the "Lady with a big heart" had meanwhile gained disc brakes and enchanted many young men all over the world ...

Right: The 2.6 liter, offered along with the 1600, had a body by Touring of Milan (Superleggera) that made the body look longer.

1966

Early round-tailed Spiders are desirable collectors' items today, even though the "Octopus" (ossi di sepia) was not too popular in terms of styling. This brochure is from 1966.

ALFA ROMEO SPIDER 1600

The new Spider 1600 is a splendid blend of elegance and power. This is the car that will renew the primacy of the "Spider" of Alfa Romeo all over the world.

IT IS THE MOST BEAUTIFUL UNDER THE SUN
The lines are a design by Pininfarina, perfectly proportioned, streamlined and beautiful. An expression of Italian styling.

At 185 kph the new Spider 1600 is among the fastest in its class. In addition, as with all Alfa Romeos, its average highway speeds are very close to its top speed, thanks to its robust motor.

Based on safety are all the characteristics of the new Spider: from its acceleration to its reserve power—at 145 kph the motor is hardly halfway to its full power. In terms of roadholding, an Alfa advantage, it is absolutely safe with its disc brakes.

The famous Alfa 5-speed gearbox is softly synchronized, with the ability to guarantee a flowing, perfect run on any road.

ER IST DER SCHÖNSTE UNTER DER SONNE

Der neue Spider 1600 ist eine grossartige Verbindung von Eleganz und Kraft. Er ist der welcher auf der ganzen Welt das Primat « Spider » von Alfa Romeo erneuern wird.

Die Linie ist ein Entwurf von Pininfarina, perfekt in den Proportionen, der Stromlinienform und der Schönheit. Ein Ausdruck italienischer Formgestaltung.

Mit 185 km/h ist der neue Spider 1600 unter den Schnellsten seiner Klasse. Ausserdem liegen, wie bei allen Alfa Romeo, seine Autostrassendurchschnittsgeschwindigkeiten, dank seines robusten Motors, sehr nahe an der Höchstgeschwindigkeit.

Auf der Sicherheit basieren alle Charakteristiken des neuen Spider: von der Beschleunigung bis zur Kraftreserve - bei 145 km/h ist der Motor kaum auf der Hälfte seiner wirklichen Leistung. Hinsichtlich der Strassenlage, ein Vorzug von Alfa, mit den Scheibenbremsen absolut sicher.

Das famose Alfa-Getriebe mit 5 Gängen: sanft synchronisiert, mit der Fähigkeit, auf jeder Strecke einen fliessenden, vollkommenen Lauf zu gewährleisten.
Der 5. Gang erlaubt das Fahren bei anhaltend

Right: the round-tailed Spider in profile. With hardtop in place, one could turn the convertible into a closed car with the snugness of a sedan. The hardtop package cost 1200 Marks.

hohen Geschwindigkeiten mit niedrigster Motorkraft und sparsamem Kraftstoffverbrauch.
Eine extreme Stabilität zeichnet das Fahrgestell aus. Motor und Aufhängungen sind so ausgelegt, um höchsten Beanspruchungen standzuhalten.
Ein aussergewöhnliches Verhältnis Leistung/Gewicht vermittelt eine Fahrbegeisterung beim Überholen, auf kurven- und steigungsreichen Strassen.
Der Komfort des Spider 1600 ist eine Neuheit, besonders hinsichtlich der Sitze. Perfekt geneigt und in richtigem Abstand angeordnet, sichern diese eine ideale Fahrposition für schnelle Reisen. Ihre anatomische Form ist vollkommen, die Flexibilität richtig. Der Gepäckraum hat eine für die anspruchsvollsten Reisen genügend grosse Geräumigkeit.
Das Hardtop verwandelt den Spider 1600 im Handumdrehen in ein Coupé: das Fahrzeug ist vollkommen was den Komfort betrifft, elegant als offener Wagen.

The 5th gear allows driving at steady high speeds with the least engine power and thrifty fuel consumption.

Extreme stability stands out in the chassis: The motor and attachments are laid out to stand up to the highest demands.

An extraordinary ratio of power to weight provides for fine acceleration when passing, on curves and steep roads.

The comfort of the Spider 1600 is a new feature, especially in terms of the seats. Perfectly angled and at the right location, they assure an ideal driving position for fast travel. Their anatomical form is just right, as is their flexibility. The luggage space is roomy enough for the most stringent travel needs.

The hardtop turns the Spider 1600 into a coupe with a twist of the wrist: the vehicle is everything in terms of comfort, and elegant as an open car.

Simple and purposeful was the dashboard. Here design changes, such as were made in the course of years, could scarcely lead to improvements . . .

27

Zylinder			4 in Reihe
Bohrung		mm	78
Hub		mm	82
Hubraum		ccm	1570
Leistung bei 6000 U/min		PS-DIN	109
		PS-SAE	125
Radstand		mm	2250
Spur vorn		mm	1310
Spur hinten		mm	1270
Länge		mm	4250
Breite		mm	1580
Höhe (unbeladen)		mm	1290
Trockengewicht		kg	940
Höchstgeschwindigkeit:		über km/h	185
Reifen			155 x 15
Elektrische Anlage		Volt	12
Tankinhalt		Liter	46
Sitzplätze			2

Vergaseranlage: 2 Doppelhorizontalvergaser

Ventilsteuerung: Die Ventilsteuerung der obenhängenden V-förmig angeordneten Ventile wird von zwei Nockenwellen über dazwischenliegende, im Ölbad gelagerte Ventilbecher direkt vorgenommen.

Kupplung: Einscheibentrockenkupplung mit Torsionsdämpfer, mit progressiver Wirkung.

Getriebe: 5 synchronisierte Vorwärtsgänge, 1 Rückwärtsgang, Knüppelschaltung.

Hinterachse: Starrachse, durch zwei an Gummilagern aufgehängte Längs-schubarme geführt. Seitliche Verankerung durch Reaktionsdreieck, das am Rahmen und an der Hinterachse in Gummipuffern gelagert ist. Der Achsantrieb hat Hypoidverzahnung

Vorderradaufhängung: Einzelradaufhängung an Querlenkern, Schraubenfedern und hidraulischen Teleskopstossdämpfern, querliegender Torsionsstab als Kurvenstabilisator.

Hinterradaufhängung: Schraubenfedern und hydraulische Teleskopstossdämpfer.

Lenkung: Kugelumlauflenkung oder mit Schnecke und Rolle.

Bremsen: 4 Scheibenbremsen, mechanische Handbremse.

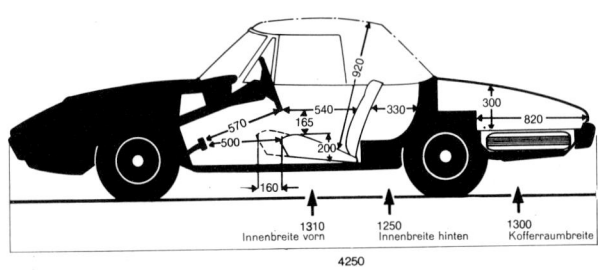

1966

Cylinders: 4 in line
Bore: 78 mm
Stroke: 82 mm
Displacement: 1570 cc
HP at 6000 rpm: 109 DIN / 125 SAE
Wheelbase: 2250 mm
Front track: 1310 mm
Rear track: 1270 mm
Length: 4250 mm

Width: 1580 mm
Height (empty): 1290 mm
Dry weight: 940 kg
Top speed: over 185 kph
Tires: 155 x 15
Electric system: 12 volt
Fuel capacity: 46 liters
Seats: 2

Carburetion: 2 double horizontal carburetors

Valve operation: The hanging valves in V formation are activated by two camshafts via intermediate cups with bearings in an oil bath.

Clutch: One-disc dry clutch with torsion spring, with progressive effect.

Gears: 5 synchronized forward speeds, 1 reverse, stick shift.

Rear Axle: Rigid axle, led by two longitudinal leading arms in rubber mounts. Lateral anchoring through reaction triangle mounted on the frame and in rubber buffers on the rear axle. The differential has hypoid gearing.

Front Suspension: Independent suspension by transverse links, coil springs and hydraulic telescopic shock absorbers, transverse torsion bar as curve stabilizer.

Rear Suspension: Coil springs and hydraulic telescopic shock absorbers.

Steering: Ball-joint or rack-and-pinion steering.

Brakes: 4 disc brakes, mechanical hand brake.

Left: Technical data of the round-tailed Spider 1600. Small errors in the text reveal that the brochure was written outside Germany (by a Milan advertising agency). Interestingly, two different steering systems are offered—here as also later.

Right: The interior of the 1600 Spider of 1966. The catalog text did not say whether the seats were covered in genuine leather. Right-hand-drive Spiders were also made by Alfa Romeo from 1966 on.

28

Right: Title page of a 1967 Spider catalog, lavishly prepared with a number of outstanding color pictures (see also the title illustration). The last interior page gives a list of Alfa Romeo's most important racing victories.

Left: One of the interior pages of the brochure described above. The pictures were taken by photographer Alessandro Garzanti.

29

It is stated convincingly in this text how sportingly one gets on with the Alfa Spider. "If they should be crowded"—meaning the country roads—"make use of four gears and an outstanding motor that allow lightning-fast passing." The safety reserve was in fact enormous, and the fifth gear, as a kind of overdrive, also a way to save fuel.

Spider: eine Höchstleistung von Alfa Romeo

Der erste von Alfa Romeo hergestellte Wagen war ein Spider, und ein Spider war der erste Alfa, der an einem Wettrennen teilnahm und gewann. Seit dieser Zeit ist der Erfolg diesen Wagen treu geblieben, die vorteilhafterweise nur 2 Sitze haben, die ideal für Reisen mit offenem Verdeck sind, die eine elegantere Linie als die anderen Wagen und gleichzeitig die Leistungsfähigkeit der echten Sportwagen aufweisen.

Die Leistungsfähigkeit Alfa Romeo bedeutet Sicherheit

Versuchen Sie einmal, den nervenraubenden Stadtverkehr, der übrigens vom Spider 1600 infolge seiner hervorragenden Elastizität glänzend gemeistert wird, hinter sich zu lassen und fahren Sie auf die Landstrasse. Sollte diese überfüllt sein, so verfügen Sie über 4 Gänge und einen hervorragenden Motor, die ein blitzartiges Überholen erlauben. Auf alle Fälle wird es nicht lange dauern, bis Sie freie Fahrt vor sich haben. Und dies ist ein für alle Wagen überraschender Augenblick: der Übergang in den fünften Gang. Sie werden nun eine andere Fahrtflüssigkeit feststellen (der Drehzahlmesser geht zurück, und nun fahren Sie unter idealen Bedingungen, d.h. Sie sparen Kraftstoff).

Diese Eigenschaft und die Tatsache, dass Ihr Motor bei 145 km/h kaum die Hälfte seiner effektiven Leistungsfähigkeit in Anspruch nimmt, sind wirklich von grösster Bedeutung. Sie können folglich mit noch höheren Leistungen rechnen und sich dementsprechend einrichten. Sie verfügen mindestens noch über ein Beschleunigungsvermögen von weiteren 40 km/h — wenn andere Wagen dieses Beschleunigungsvermögen nicht einmal im dritten Gang aufweisen — und besitzen folglich eine Reserve, die Sicherheit bedeutet und die jeder gute Fahrer im geeigneten Moment mit der gleichen Wirkung eines schnellen Bremsens zu verwenden weiss.

Spider: a high achievement by Alfa Romeo

The first car made by Alfa Romeo was a Spider, and the first Alfa that took part in a race and won was a Spider. Since that time success has remained true to these cars, which advantageously have only two seats that are ideal for top-down motoring, a more elegant styling than other cars, and at the same time the high-performance capability of true sports cars.

High-Performance Alfa Romeo means safety

Try leaving the nerve-wracking city traffic behind, that is mastered splendidly by the Spider 1600 thanks to its outstanding flexibility, and drive out onto the country roads. If they should be crowded, make use of four gears and an outstanding motor that allow lightning-fast passing. In any case, it won't be long till you have an open road ahead of you. And this is an amazing moment in any car: shifting into fifth gear. You will now feel a different fluidity to driving (the tachometer drops back, and now you drive under ideal conditions, which means you save gasoline).

This quality and the fact that your motor is scarcely using half its effective potential power at 145 kph are really of the greatest importance. They mean you can count on even higher performance and handle the car accordingly. You still have the potential to increase your speed by another 40 kph—which other cars don't even have in third gear—and thus you have a reserve that means safety, and that every good driver knows how to use along with the equal effect of fast braking.

1966

Left: The chocolate-like side of the Spider 1600, at that time with plexiglas covers on the headlights. The small emblems on the rear of Italian cars are always recognized with envy in other European lands by those who have to get along with emblems that spoil the lines of their cars . . .

Right: One is referred to the driving skills of Nuvolari, Fangio and Sanesi, to stress the safety of an Alfa Romeo. The experience gained in building racing cars flows into series production, which has always gone without saying.

The fact that average speeds can be maintained on superhighways points to very great performance potential. The capability of immediate acceleration in all gears can be attributed to the precise adjustment of the two double horizontal carburetors.

Roadholding proved on the racecourse

The temptation to race is very great with a Spider 1600. But all Alfa Romeos are built precisely for high speeds, since they can handle any acceleration thanks to their special construction and weight distribution that holds the car on the road in difficult situations. There are actually very few cars that can inspire so much trust. Straight stretches and curves roll by under the wheels as if the tires had been designed with rulers and compasses. The Alfa Romeo does not skid or slide, and gives the impression above all that the car never fails; and this gives the driver and passengers a feeling of security and calm.

But let us presume that braking is unavoidable.

What moves must also be brought to a stop, and to be sure, immediately and unconditionally, no matter what the surface or the speed. Quick braking will always remain a pleasant surprise for all passengers in Alfa Romeos: the car reacts unfailingly, and in fact, more and more strongly until it stops completely. Not only the art of the technicians contributes to this, but also the experience gained in racing by Nuvolari, Fangio and Sanesi.

Die Tatsache, dass auf Autobahnen durchschnittliche Geschwindigkeiten, eingehalten werden können, deutet auf eine sehr grosse Leistungsfähigkeit hin. Das sofortige Beschleunigungsvermögen in allen Gängen ist der genauen Einstellung der beiden doppelten Horizontalvergaser zu verdanken.

Eine auf den Pisten bewährte Strassenlage

Die Versuchung zu rasen ist mit einem Spider 1600 sehr gross. Alle Alfa Romeo sind aber gerade für hohe Geschwindigkeiten gebaut, da diese dank ihrer besonderen Strukturen jeglicher Beschleunigung und einer Gewichteverteilung, die den Wagen in schwierigen Situationen auf der Strasse hält, standhalten. Wirklich nur wenige Wagen wissen ein solches Vertrauen einzuflössen. Geradlinige Strecken und Kurven prägen sich unter den Reifen so ein, als ob diese mit dem Lineal und dem Zirkel gezeichnet worden wären. Die Alfa Romeo kennen kein Rutschen und kein Schlittern und vermitteln vor allem den Eindruck, dass der Wagen nie versagt: und dies gibt dem Fahrer und den Fahrgästen Sicherheit und Ruhe.

Nehmen wir jedoch einmal an, dass ein Bremsen unvermeidlich ist

Was läuft muss auch zum Anhalten gebracht werden können, und zwar sofort und einwandfrei, gleich auf welchem Boden oder bei welcher Geschwindigkeit. Ein schnelles Bremsen wird für alle im Alfa Romeo reisenden Fahrgäste immer eine freudige Überraschung bleiben: der Wagen reagiert unfehlbar und zwar immer stärker und stärker bis zum vollkommenen Stillstand. Dazu gehören nicht nur die Kunst der Techniker sondern auch die Erfahrungen, die bei den Rennen der Nuvolari, Fangio und Sanesi gesammelt wurden.

Giulia Sprint GTC

The term "Sprint" formerly applied only to the coupes bodied by Bertone, but an exception was made for the open GTC. Barely 500 of these cars were made from 1965 to the end of 1966—a 180-kph car.

Alfa Romeo Modelle 1966/67

Motor: 4-cylinder 4-stroke in-line
Bore: 78 mm
Stroke: 82 mm
Displacement: 1570 cc
HP at 6000 rpm: 102 HP
Crankshaft: 5 bearings
Wheelbase: 2350 mm
Front track: 1310 mm
Rear track: 1270 mm
Length: 4080 mm
Width: 1580 mm
Height (unladen): 1315 mm
Dry weight: 950 kg
Top speed: more than 180 kph
Tires: 155 x 15
Seats: 4
Electric system: 12-volt
Fuel capacity: 46 liters

CARBURETION: 2 double horizontal carburetors
VALVE OPERATION: activation of the natrium-cooled dropped valves in V formation by two overhead camshafts via intermediate cups in oil bath
CLUTCH: One-plate dry clutch with torsion damper, with progressive effect
GEARBOX: 5 synchronized forward and 1 reverse gears, stick shift
REAR AXLE: Rigid axle, led by two longitudinal leading arms mounted in rubber mounts. Lateral anchoring by reaction triangle attached by rubber buffers to the frame and rear axle. The axle drive has hypoid gearing
FRONT SUSPENSION: Independent suspension by transverse links, coil springs and hydraulic telescopic shock absorbers. Transverse torsion bar as curve stabilizer
REAR SUSPENSION: Coil springs and hydraulic telescopic shock absorbers
STEERING: Ball-joint or rack-and-pinion steering
BRAKES: 4 disc brakes, servo braking assistance. Mechanical hand brake
STANDARD EQUIPMENT (at no extra cost): Belted tires, safety glass windshield, tachometer, flashers, backup light, windshield washers, daily odometer

Motor	Vierzylinder-Viertakt-Reihenmotor	Länge	4080 mm
Bohrung	78 mm	Breite	1580 mm
Hub	82 mm	Höhe (unbeladen)	1315 mm
Hubraum	1570 ccm	Trockengewicht	950 kg
Leistung bei 6000 U/min	102 PS	Höchstgeschwindigkeit mehr als	180 km/h
Kurbelwelle	fünffach gelagert	Reifen	155 x 15
		Sitzplätze	4
Radstand	2350 mm	elektrische Anlage	12 V
Spurweite vorn	1310 mm	Tankinhalt	46 l
Spurweite hinten	1270 mm		

VERGASERANLAGE: 2 Doppelhorizontalvergaser
VENTILSTEUERUNG: Die Ventilsteuerung der obenhängenden, V-förmig angeordneten, natriumgekühlten Ventile wird von zwei Nockenwellen über dazwischenliegende, im Ölbad gelagerte Ventilbecher direkt vorgenommen
KUPPLUNG: Einscheibentrockenkupplung mit Torsionsdämpfern, mit progressiver Wirkung
GETRIEBE: 5 synchronisierte Vorwärtsgänge und 1 Rückwärtsgang. Knüppelschaltung
HINTERACHSE: Starrachse, durch zwei an Gummilagern aufgehängte Längsschubarme geführt. Seitliche Verankerung durch Reaktionsdreieck, das am Rahmen und an der Hinterachse in Gummipuffern gelagert ist. Der Achsantrieb hat Hypoidverzahnung
VORDERRADAUFHÄNGUNG: Einzelradaufhängung an Querlenkern, Schraubenfedern und hydraulischen Teleskop-Stoßdämpfern. Querliegender Torsionsstab als Kurvenstabilisator
HINTERRADAUFHÄNGUNG: Schraubenfedern und hydraulische Teleskopstoßdämpfer
LENKUNG: Kugelumlauflenkung oder mit Schnecke und Rolle
BREMSEN: 4 Scheibenbremsen. Servo-Bremshilfe. Mechanische Handbremse
SERIENMÄSSIGE AUSSTATTUNG (ohne Mehrpreis): Gürtelreifen, Verbundglasscheibe, Drehzahlmesser, Lichthupe, Rückfahrscheinwerfer, Scheibenwaschanlage, Tageskilometerzähler

Giulia Sprint GTC

Left: The GTC (C for Cabriolet: convertible) was made only in small numbers and was one of the last open cars that Touring built for Alfa. The GTC made its debut at the 1965 Geneva Salon (but production started just before 1965 began). Technically, the car corresponded to the 1600 T or 1600 GTV.

Motor: 4-cylinder 4-stroke in-line
Bore: 78 mm
Stroke: 82 mm
Displacement: 1570 cc
HP at 6000 rpm: 109 HP
Crankshaft: 5 bearings
Wheelbase: 2250 mm
Front track: 1310 mm
Rear track: 1270 mm
Length: 4250 mm
Width: 1630 mm
Height: 1290 mm
Dry weight: 940 kg
Top speed: over 185 kph
Tires: 155 x 15
Seats: 2
Electric system: 12-volt
Fuel capacity: 46 liters

The "osso di sepia" (octopus) concept for the round-tailed Spider, before the 1600 was named "Duetto", was actually used only unofficially. Yet this term is found as the usual name of the type in a 1966 German-language brochure.

Motor	Vierzylinder-Viertakt-Reihenmotor	Spurweite hinten	1270 mm
Bohrung	78 mm	Länge	4250 mm
Hub	82 mm	Breite	1630 mm
Hubraum	1570 ccm	Höhe	1290 mm
Leistung bei 6000 U/min	109 PS	Trockengewicht	940 kg
Kurbelwelle	fünffach gelagert	Höchstgeschwindigkeit üb.	185 km/h
		Reifen	155 x 15
		Sitzplätze	2
Radstand	2250 mm	elektrische Anlage	12 V
Spurweite vorn	1310 mm	Tankinhalt	46 l

VERGASERANLAGE: 2 Doppelhorizontalvergaser
VENTILSTEUERUNG: Die Ventilsteuerung der obenhängenden, V-förmig angeordneten Ventile wird von zwei Nockenwellen über dazwischenliegende, im Ölbad gelagerte Ventilbecher direkt vorgenommen
KUPPLUNG: Einscheibentrockenkupplung mit Torsionsdämpfern in progressiver Wirkung
GETRIEBE: 5 synchronisierte Vorwärtsgänge und 1 Rückwärtsgang. Knüppelschaltung
HINTERACHSE: Starrachse, durch zwei an Gummilagern aufgehängte Längsschubarme geführt. Seitliche Verankerung durch Reaktionsdreieck, das am Rahmen und an der Hinterachse in Gummipuffern gelagert ist. Der Achsantrieb hat Hypoidverzahnung
VORDERRADAUFHÄNGUNG: Einzelradaufhängung an Querlenkern, Schraubenfedern und hydraulischen Teleskop-Stoßdämpfern. Querliegender Torsionsstab als Kurvenstabilisator
HINTERRADAUFHÄNGUNG: Schraubenfedern und hydraulische Teleskopstoßdämpfer
LENKUNG: Kugelumlauflenkung oder mit Schnecke und Rolle
BREMSEN: 4 Scheibenbremsen. Mechanische Handbremse
SERIENMÄSSIGE AUSSTATTUNG (ohne Mehrpreis): Gürtelreifen, Verbundglasscheibe, Drehzahlmesser, Lichthupe, Rückfahrscheinwerfer, Scheibenwaschanlage, Tageskilometerzähler

Osso di Sepia

1750 Spider Veloce

In 1967 Alfa Romeo introduced the 1750 Spider, which also bore the name "Veloce" from the start. This car remained in Alfa's program until the end of 1971. The round-tailed bodywork was retained at first; the technical concept was identical to that of the 1600 except for the larger engine displacement. In 1970 the Spider 1750 also was given a notchback, and many Alfa fans welcomed this heartily—even though the luggage space had increased only slightly in the process.

Production of the new 1750 began at the end of 1967. With a slightly longer wheelbase it was a stylistically overdone car, capable of 190 kph in Spider form.

1968

Red is not only the national racing color of Italy but also the house color of Alfa Romeo. In 1968 this little catalog was issued for the Brussels Auto Show.

The technical data of the 1750 Spider, officially introduced in 1968. The car was fitted with disc brakes. Dual-circuit brake systems and fuel injection were reserved for the USA export models.

Spider 1750 Technical Data
Cylinders: 4 in line
Bore: 80 mm
Stroke: 88.5 mm
Displacement: 1779 cc
HP at 5500 rpm: 132 SAE HP
Wheelbase: 2250 mm
Front track: 1324 mm
Rear track: 1274 mm
Length: 4250 mm
Width: 1630 mm
Height (unladen): 1290 mm
Ready-to-drive weight: 1040 kg
Top speed: 190 kph
Tires: 165 x 14
Seats: 2
Electric system: 12-volt
Fuel capacity: 46 liters

Carburetion: 2 double horizontal carburetors.

Valve operation: The dropped valves in V-formation are activated by two overhead camshafts via intermediate cups in an oil bath. Natrium-cooled valves.

Clutch: Single-plate dry clutch with torsion damper, with progressive effect. Hydraulically activated membrane spring.

Gearbox: 5 synchronized forward and 1 reverse gears, stick shift.

Rear axle: Rigid axle, led by two longitudinal leading arms mounted in rubber mounts. Lateral anchoring by reaction triangle mounted in rubber buffers on frame and rear axle. Differential has hypoid gearing.

Front suspension: Independent suspension by rectangular transverse links, coil springs and hydraulic telescopic shock absorbers, transverse torsion bar as curve stabilizer.

Rear suspension: Coil springs and hydraulic telescopic shock absorbers, transverse torsion bar as curve stabilizer.

Steering: Ball-joint or rack-and-pinion steering.

Brakes: 4 disc brakes with power assistance. Power brake regulation on the rear wheels. Hand brake independent of main braking system, working on rear brake drums.

34

1300 Junior Spider

In May of 1968 a thrifty version came on the market, the 1300 in convertible form, which thoroughly represented the traditional Alfa Romeo line in its technical conception, but was more economical with its proven 1290 cc motor and could be had for a considerably more reasonable price. The Spider 1300 became a sales success at once, even though it did not equal the sales figures of the 1750. At first the "little" Junior Spider too was a round-tailed car, but in the course of restyling the whole Alfa line it became a notchback.

Two pages of a lavishly prepared catalog for the 1300 Junior introduced in 1968. Who would not work up an appetite for driving an open car?

1968

1969

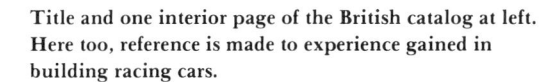

Title and one interior page of the British catalog at left. Here too, reference is made to experience gained in building racing cars.

Style. This is a classical « Italian » design: a miracle of elegance, aerodynamics and comfort.

The exterior of the car is a continuous flow of curves, giving air penetration and road holding qualities that have been tested at very high speeds and in very tough races. The new version of this model incorporates the « cut-off rear » feature, which gives greater style and a better line to the vehicle.

The long wheelbase and low centre of gravity are essential sports car features. And the interior gives a degree of driving comfort — and of passenger relaxation — which are invariable at any speed. The seats are body-supporting, adjustable and reclinable. Comfort is assured not only by the anatomical suitability of the driver's position, but also by the careful design of the suspension and the quality of the fittings. As with any Alfa Romeo, the instruments are complete in every respect, and are easy to read and of elegant design.

The problem of the boot — a difficult one in the case of sports cars — has here been solved. Its shape — with a capacity of 5 cub. ft. — has been moulded so as to accommodate full-sized suitcases: and as many of them as are needed for two on a long journey. The hood folds back completely and in winter can be replaced by a hard-top, for which provision was made in the original design of the car and thus is both functional and elegant.

Left: Two pages from an opulent catalog for the 1300 Junior at the end of 1968. It does not include a picture of the entire car, uncut—only: cropped pictures and detail photos, the effect of which is all the more brilliant. The factory did not give it plexiglas covers over the headlights. And the rear design corresponds with that of the 1750.

37

SPIDER JUNIOR

Details from the 1968-69 catalog for the 1300 Spider. It was redone in 1970 and 1971. The photos come from the studio of Gastone Jung—no more outdoor shots of speeding cars with pretty girls and muscular men.

1300

1969

The Spider 1300 was reasonably priced but not cheap. It cost 13,600 Marks; a Morgan Plus 8 cost somewhat more than 15,000. But the latter also had 16-month delivery.

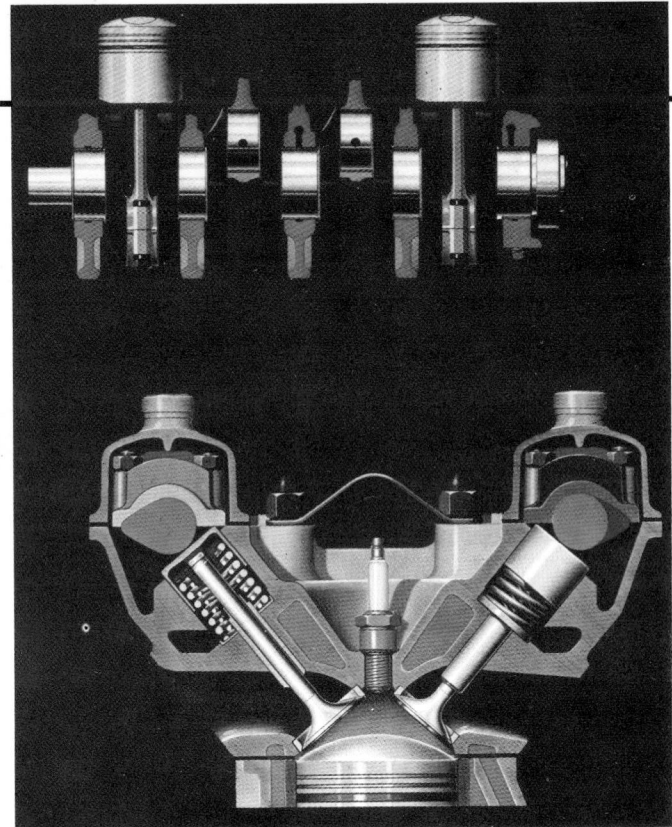

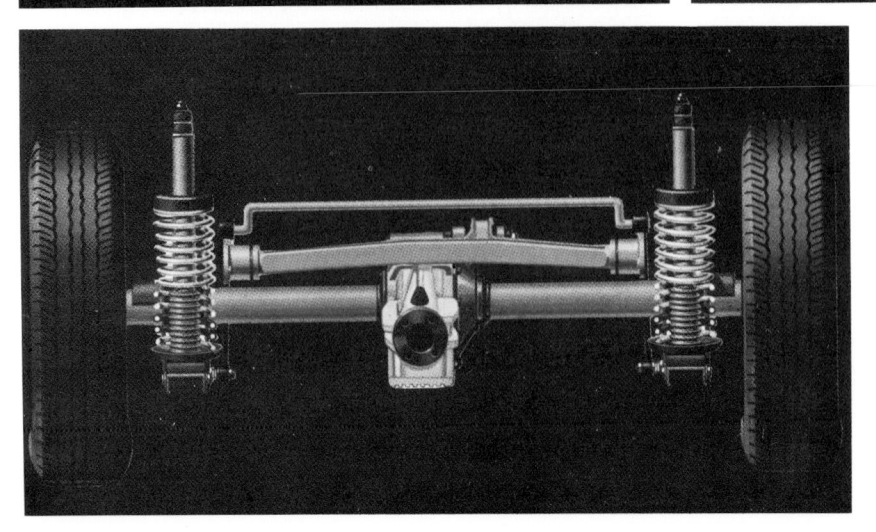

Technical details, portrayed in the 1969 catalog described on the previous page. The two overhead camshafts had been a firm tradition at Alfa for forty years.

In June of 1971 the Spider 2000 came out—a really long-lived car that could still be bought in scarcely changed form, other than a face-lifting operation, early in 1986. The dohc motor displaced 1962 cc and produced 150 SAE or 132 DIN horsepower.

Left: Intimate look—the interior of the Spider 2000 Veloce. At first glance the cockpit does not look at all different from that of the previous model. Compare pages 28 and 37!

Reference was made to the close relationship between the Two-liter and the GTAm, which was after all a very successful racing car. In 1971 and 1972 2728 of the 2000 Spider were built.

Vom GT/Am die Leistung der neuen 2000 GT Veloce und Spider Veloce

From the GT/Am the power of the new 2000 GT Veloce and Spider Veloce

The new 2000 GT Veloce and Spider Veloce are famous from the start of their existence, because they developed from the Alfa Romeo GT/Am, the winner of the European Touring Car Championship in 1970, and utilize all the advantages of the proven 1750 model. Because they are even more powerful, safer and more comfortable. They set a new high standard for all sports cars in the same category.

Die neuen 2000 GT Veloce und Spider Veloce sind schon von Beginn ihrer Existenz an berühmt, weil sie aus dem ALFA ROMEO GT/Am hervorgegangen sind, dem Gewinner der Europa-Tourenwagen-Meisterschaft 1970 und sich alle Vorzüge des bewährten Modells 1750 zunutze machen. Weil sie noch leistungsfähiger, noch sicherer und noch komfortabler sind. Sie stellen einen neuen hohen Vergleichsmassstab dar für alle sportlichen Wagen gleicher Kategorie.

1971-75

Komfort

Einer der besonderen Vorzüge des 2000 GT Veloce ist, dass er den Reisenden in hohem Masse Komfort bietet, ohne dass sein sportlicher Charakter dadurch beeinträchtigt würde.

Er ist stabil, hat also eine gute Strassenlage in jedem Fahrbereich. Durch seine gute Federung lässt es sich in ihm bequem reisen. Schliesslich fährt er sehr ruhig.

Der Fahrerplatz ist ein richtiges Cockpit. Sämtliche Kontrollinstrumente sind gut zu übersehen und die Bedienungshebel leicht zu betätigen. Das Lenkrad ist aus Holz, in seinen Speichen ist die Hupe eingebaut. Die körpergerecht geformten und komfortablen Sitze sind verstellbar.

Die hintere Sitzbank bietet zwei Personen Platz. Der wirklich hohe Reisekomfort wird noch vervollständigt durch eine 2-stufige Klimaanlage sowie einen geräumigen Kofferraum.

Comfort

One of the special advantages of the 2000 GT Veloce is that it offers travelers a high degree of comfort without detracting from its sporting character.

It is stable, thus has good roadholding in any type of driving. With its good suspension, it lets you ride comfortably in it. And it also rides very quietly.

The driver's seat is a real cockpit. All the control instruments are easy to see, and the control levers are easy to reach. The steering wheel is made of wood, with the horn built into its spokes. The comfortable seats, designed with the body in mind, are adjustable.

The rear seat offers room for two people. The really high degree of travel comfort is completed by a 2-stage air conditioner as well as roomy luggage space.

Left: The accessories industry always offered many extras to sporting Italians. But a light metal alternative with spoke effect for the 2000 Spider Veloce could be had right from the factory.

Right: The interior of the 2000 corresponded to that of the 1750. The strongly shaded instruments, the console in the center of the car, and the three-spoke steering wheel were the same. But: the heater/ventilator knob was now matt black instead of chromed.

43

Below: the strong heart of the 2000 Veloce. It produced 132 HP and was fed by two double horizontal carburetors. The exhaust valves were natrium-cooled.

The design comes from Pininfarina; it is a successful blend of esthetics and purposefulness.

Its comfort fully matches its achievements.

Praise belongs first to its stability, which is excellent in every kind of driving. Then the arrangement and form of the seats, which make even the longest trips pleasant. They are formed to fit the body and enclose the body correctly; they are provided with mounts for headrests. And they have just the right springs. Running on rails, they can be moved forward or back, the seat backs are adjustable, so everyone can create the seat position best suited to his size. Two more people find seats in back.

Instruments and furnishings are such as one can expect from a luxury car and a high-class body. The dashboard and the steering wheel are particularly elegant. Suitcases can indeed be stowed in the luggage space; usually one must do without this in a Spider.

Finally, it is especially important that a car in which one can fully enjoy fresh air and sunshine should also provide protection against rain and coldness. The top, which can be raised easily, is sufficient for the former. To keep out the cold, a firm roof (hardtop) is intended, which turns the Spider into a coupe that is just as elegant and comfortable as the open car.

Der Entwurf stammt von Pininfarina; es ist eine glückliche Mischung von Aesthetik und Zweckdienlichkeit.

Sein Komfort entspricht voll seinen Leistungen.

Ein erstes Lob gebührt natürlich seiner Stabilität, die in jedem Fahrbereich ausgezeichnet ist. Dann der Anordnung und der Form der Sitze, durch die sich auch die längsten Reisen angenehm gestalten. Sie sind körpergerecht geformt und hüllen den Körper förmlich ein; sie sind mit Verankerungen für Kopfstützen versehen. Dazu haben sie genau die richtige Federung. Auf Schienen laufend lassen sie sich nach vorn oder hinten schieben, die Rückenlehnen sind neigbar, ein jeder kann sich also die für seine Körpergrösse am besten geeignete Sitzposition schaffen. Hinten finden zwei weitere Personen Platz.

Instrumente und Ausstattung sind so, wie man sie bei einem Luxuswagen und einer Karosserie von Klasse erwarten kann. Besonders elegant sind das Armaturenbrett und auch das Lenkrad. Im Kofferraum lassen sich wirklich Gepäckstücke unterbringen; gewöhnlich muss man darauf bei einem Spider verzichten.

Schliesslich ist es besonders wichtig, dass ein Wagen, in welchem man Luft und Sonne voll geniessen kann, auch Schutz bietet gegen Regen und Kälte. Für ersteres genügt das Planenverdeck, das sich mit einem Griff hochmachen lässt. Gegen Kälte jedoch ist ein festes Verdeck (Hardtop) vorgesehen, das den Spider in ein Coupé verwandelt, welches ebenso komfortabel und elegant ist wie der offene Wagen.

Above: Double page from the same brochure for the 2000 GT Veloce/Spider Veloce models, 1971-73. What was spoken of in the advertisement: deforming areas, halogen headlights, pressure-release valve—it was supposed to help avoid locking the rear wheels.

1971-75

Below: Safety through technology—a slogan gladly taken up by other auto manufacturers too. Quite in place at Alfa.

Die Alfa-Romeo-Technik bedeutet Sicherheit
In mancher Beziehung eilt Alfa Romeo anderen Automobilproduzenten voraus. Spitzengeschwindigkeit, Beschleunigung, Strassenlage, Bremsen: es sind dies Vorzüge, die man bei jedem Alfa Romeo vorfindet. Hinzu kommen der mässige Verbrauch, die Geräuscharmut und der Komfort.
Diese Vorzüge führen, dank der höheren Leistungsfähigkeit des Wagens und dem ruhigeren Fahrgefühl für den Fahrer, zu einer grossen Fahrsicherheit.

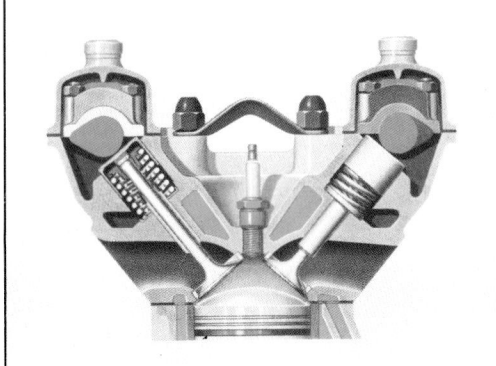

The Alfa Romeo technology means safety
In many ways Alfa Romeo races ahead of other automobile builders. Top speed, acceleration, roadholding, brakes: these are advantages that one finds in every Alfa Romeo. Along with them go the moderate fuel consumption, the quietness and the comfort.

These advantages, thanks to the higher capability of the car and the feeling of more restful driving for the driver, lead to greater driving safety.

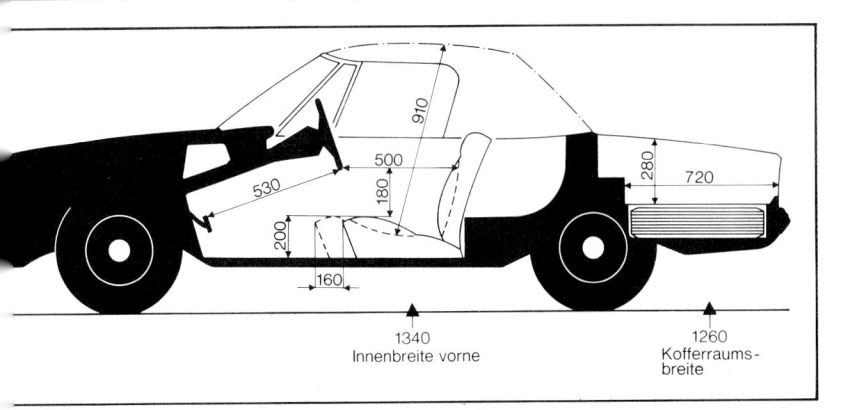

Front interior width   Trunk width

1971-75

With the same displacement, an Alfa Romeo is more powerful
The compression ratio of an Alfa Romeo is 9 to 1. This does not achieve any excessively high value, but gives a guarantee of durability. The compression of an Alfa Romeo motor is not above today's typical average. On the other hand, the specific power of an Alfa Romeo is above average.

The reasons for it are as follows:
The fuel lines are so designed that losses are reduced optimally. The mixture flows directly into the combustion chamber, and the cylinders are completely filled.

The operation of the valves occurs directly by means of two overhead camshafts, without intermediate parts such as pushrods and rockers, which cannot guarantee such precise and continuing functioning.

The extent of the flame and the total burning occur directly and without any delay, because the combustion chambers are hemispherical in form. The spark plug is in the center of the chamber. The exhaust flows out through especially well-constructed exhaust pipes that are made as precisely as the intake pipes.

Direct and complete cylinder filling, optimal combustion, quick outflow of the exhaust; these are the reasons why the power per liter is always higher with Alfa Romeo motors. The intensive combustion also results in typically moderate fuel consumption in Alfa Romeo powerplants.

The high performance of Alfa Romeo motors is not concentrated in the area over 4500 rpm. It is divided in good proportions over all engine speeds, where one can also count on the excellent support of the five-speed gearbox. An Alfa Romeo has a very high top speed, and is able to reach this speed in the shortest time. At the traffic light the car accelerates lightning-fast, and passing maneuvers can be done quickly.

The fifth gear is an additional Alfa Romeo advantage, because it amounts to an extra overdrive gear.

Naturally, the fifth gear is also meant to save fuel on superhighway driving; but here it acts first of all as a genuine gear, with which one accelerates to meet the demands of today's driving, when one must accelerate even when driving at high speeds on the superhighway.

Despite higher performance, an Alfa Romeo is durable
The top engine speed of Alfa Romeo motors is between 5000 and 6000 rpm. This is a speed that does not unduly strain the motor, so that long distances can be covered at top speed. It is to be considered too that Alfa Romeos are able to hold a very high speed at 4000 to 4500 rpm.

The crankshaft has five bearings and does not vibrate even at very high engine speed. When the motor is kept as "cool" as possible, it gives its maximum performance as long as you want:
- The Alfa Romeo motors lose heat quickly because the engine block, cylinder head and oilpan too are not made of cast iron but of a light metal alloy.
- The cylinder liners are directly surrounded by cooling water.
- The temperature of the inlet valves remains constant within a limited area, because these valves are filled with natrium.

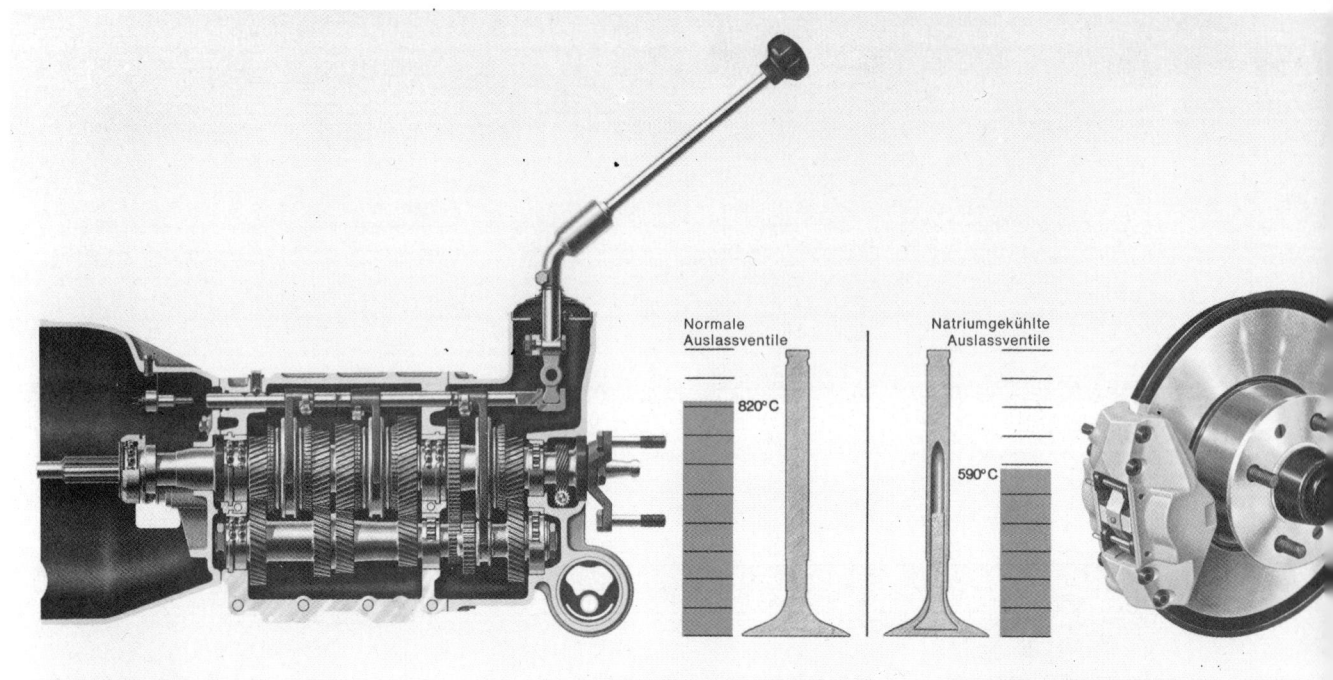

Bei gleichem Hubraum ist ein Alfa Romeo leistungsstärker
Das Verdichtungsverhältnis eines Alfa Romeo beträgt 9 : 1. Damit erreicht man keinen überaus hohen Wert, aber die Gewähr für Dauerhaftigkeit wird gegeben. Die Verdichtung eines Alfa-Romeo-Motors liegt nicht über den heute üblichen Durchschnittswerten. Hingegen ist die spezifische Leistung eines Alfa Romeo überdurchschnittlich.

Die Gründe dafür sind folgende:
Die Ansaugkanäle sind so konzipiert, dass Verluste optimal reduziert werden. Das Gemisch strömt unmittelbar in den Brennraum, die Zylinder werden restlos gefüllt.

Die Steuerung der Ventile erfolgt direkt mittels zweier obenliegender Nockenwellen, ohne dazwischenliegende mechanische Teile wie Stössel und Kipphebel, welche keinen so präzisen und kontinuiedlichen Betrieb gewährleisten.

Die Ausdehnung der Flamme und auch die totale Verbrennung erfolgen unmittelbar und ohne jegliche Verzögerung, weil die Verbrennungsräume halbkugelförmig ausgebildet sind. Die Kerze befindet sich in der Mitte des Brennraumes. Das Abgas strömt durch besonders gut durchkonstruierte Auspuffrohre, die genau so präzis wie die Ansaugrohre ausgebildet sind.

Unmittelbare und komplete Zylinderfüllung, optimale Verbrennung, schneller Austritt der Abgase: dies sind die Gründe, warum die Literleistung bei den Alfa-Romeo-Motoren immer höher ist. Die intensive Verbrennung hat auch den bei Alfa-Romeo-Aggregaten typisch mässigen Verbrauch zur Folge.

Die hohe Leistung der Alfa-Romeo-Motoren ist nicht im Bereich über 4500 U/Min konzentriert. Sie verteilt sich bei guter Proportionierung auf alle Drehzahlbereiche, wobei man zudem auf die hervorragende Unterstützung des Fünfganggetriebs zählen kann. Ein Alfa Romeo weist eine sehr hohe Spitzengeschwindigkeit auf; dieses Tempo vermag er auch in kürzester Zeit zu erreichen. Bei der Verkehrsampel beschleunigt der Wagen blitzartig, Ueberholmanöver lassen sich schnell durchführen.

Der fünfte Gang ist ein weiterer Vorzug von Alfa Romeo, weil es sich nicht um einen zusätzlichen Gang (Schongang) handelt.

Selbstverständlich soll der fünfte Gang bei Autobahnfahrten auch sparen helfen: aber hier handelt es sich in erster Linie um einen richtigen Gang, mit dem beschleunigt wird, der den heutigen Anforderungen des Verkehrs entspricht, wo auf Autobahnen bei hohem Tempo noch beschleunigt werden muss.

Trotz höheren Fahrleistungen ist ein Alfa Romeo dauerhaft
Die Höchstdrehzahl der Alfa-Romeo-Motoren lie 5000 bis 6000 U/Min. Dies ist ein Bereich, de Motor nicht stark beansprucht, so dass grosse D zen im Höchsttempo zurückgelegt werden könne sei noch berücksichtigt, dass die Alfa Romeos ei hohes Reisetempo bei 4000 bis 4500 U/Min. ein ten vermögen.

Die Kurbelwelle ist fünffach gelagert, sie vibrier bei sehr hohen Drehzahlen nicht. Wenn der Moto glichst « kühl » gehalten wird, gibt er seine ma Leistung beliebig lange ab:

- Die Alfa-Romeo-Motoren geben die Wärme s ab, weil Motorblock, Zylinderkopf wie auch Oel nicht aus Graussguss, sondern aus einer Leichtm gierung bestehen.

- Die Zylinderlaufbüchsen werden unmittelba Kühlwasser umspült.

- Die Temperatur der Auslassventile bleibt stän einem beschränkten Rahmen, weil diese Venti triumgefüllt sind.

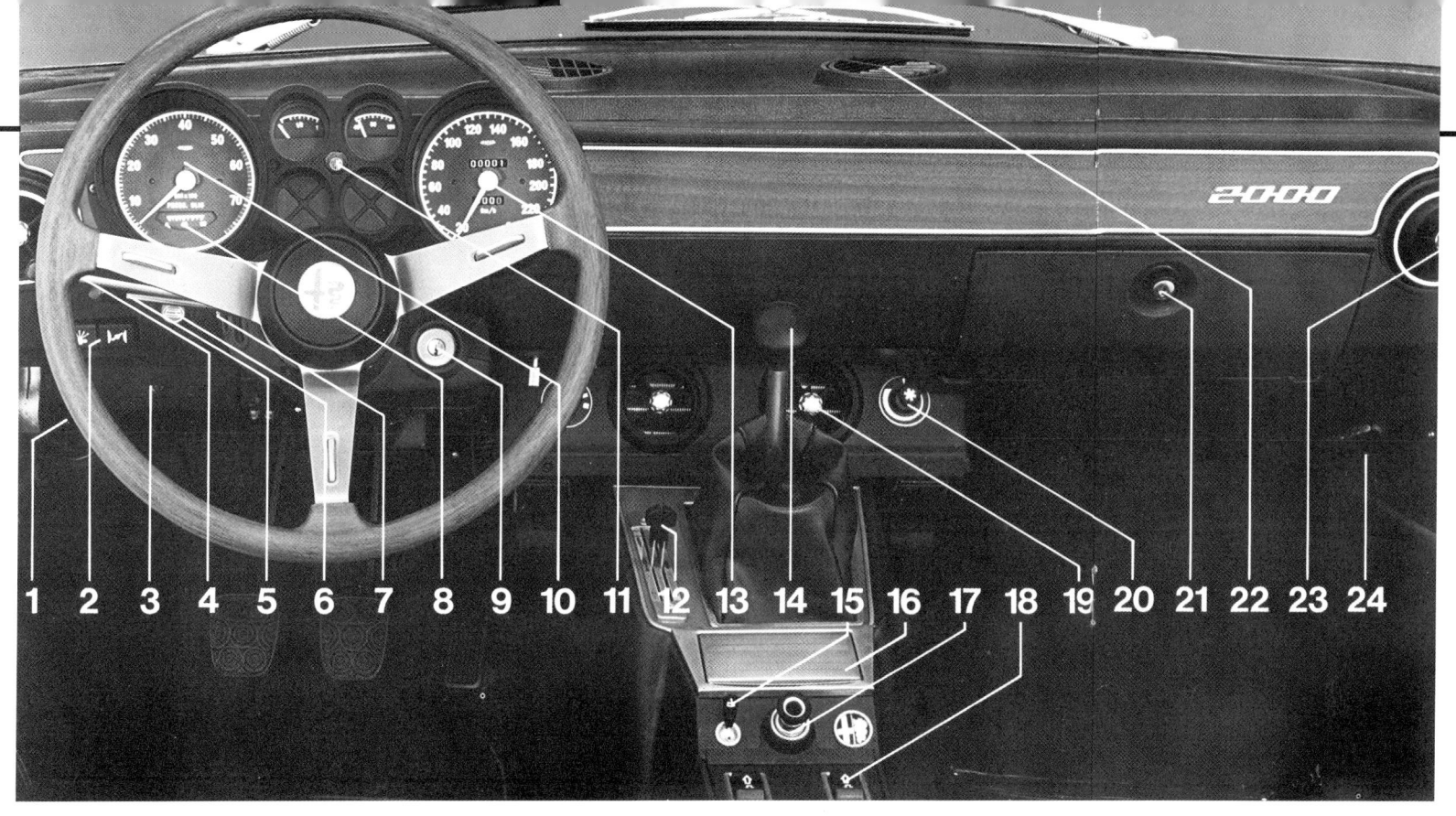

Left: Much technical information is in this brochure too. The production 2000—like all previous Alfas—had a five-speed gearbox, but also a self-locking differential!

A side trip into the cockpit of the 2000 Veloce Coupe. The instruments are arranged somewhat differently, just as the outward appearance is strikingly different.

1) Windshield washer control
2) Starter and hand throttle
3) Fuse box
4) Light and flasher switch
5) Directional light lever
6) Rear window defroster and warning light
7) Dashboard light switch
8) Oil pressure gauge
9) Starter and steering wheel lock
10) Tachometer
11) Fuel gauge and reserve tank warning light. Oil pressure warning light. Indicator lights for outside lights, hand brake, brake fluid, high beams, directionals, starter, fan, and generator, water temperature gauge.
12) Heater, ventilator and defroster controls
13) Speedometer, overall and daily odometers
14) Gearshift lever
15) Windshield wiper switch (2-speed)
16) Ashtray
17) Automatic cigarette lighter
18) Electric window control (special equipment)
19) Air conditioner ducts (special equipment)
20) Air conditioner control
21) Lockable glove compartment
22) Windshield defroster ducts
23) Fresh air ducts
24) Stowage compartment

1) Scheibenwaschanlage und -Scheibenwischer-Betätigung
2) Starter und Handgashebel
3) Sicherungskasten
4) Aussenbeleuchtung und Lichthupe
5) Blinkleuchten
6) Schalter und Kontrollampe für heizbare Heckscheibe
7) Instrumenten-Beleuchtung
8) Öldruckmesser
9) Anlasser und Lenkradschloss
10) Drehzahlmesser
11) Kraftstoff-Vorratsanzeiger und Warnleuchte für Reserveanzeige. Öldruck-Warnleuchte. Kontrollampe für Aussenbeleuchtung. Kontrolleuchte für gezogene Handbremse und Anzeige des Mindestvorrats an Bremsflüssigkeit. Kontrollampe für Blinker. Starter-Kontrolleuchte. Kontrolleuchte für Gebläse. Kontrolleuchte für Lichtmaschine. Wasserthermometer.
12) Regulierung von Heizung, Lüftung und Entfrostung
13) Geschwindigkeitsmesser. Gesamt- und Tages-Kilometerzähler
14) Getriebe-Schalthebel
15) Scheibenwischer-Betätigung (2-stufig schaltbar)
16) Aschenbecher
17) Automatischer Zigaretten-Anzünder
18) Elektrische Fensterheber (Sonderausstattung)
19) Luftdüsen der Klimaanlage (Sonderausstattung)
20) Regulierung der Klimaanlage
21) Verschliessbarer Handschuhkasten
22) Entfrosterdüsen für Windschutzscheibe
23) Frischluftdüsen
24) Tasche zum Aufbewahren von Gegenständen

47

1972   The 1600 Renaissance

Above: 1972 price list.
Right: 1972 Spider Veloce 2-liter, an Alfa Romeo advertising photo.

The 1750 Spider Veloce, on its way out in 1972, was replaced in a smooth transition by a 1600 descendant. Along with the 2-liter model, this convertible led the Alfa Romeo tradition of open two-seat sports cars into the Eighties. The proven powerplant with dual overhead camshafts delivered 103 HP at 5500 rpm, good for more than 175 kph. Disc brakes all around and a five-speed gearbox had long been taken for granted for Alfa. The Milan firm could also depend on a loyal body of customers; talking of an "Alfa virus" was not so farfetched at all: Whoever picked it up did not get rid of it soon!

1980

Spider

Alfa Romeo

Right: Title page of a nicely formed catalog of 1980. It includes several foldout double pages with brilliant photos.

Der Spider vermittelt Ihnen ein ganz neues und angenehmes Fahrgefühl: Den direkten Kontakt mit der Natur, mit Sonne und Wind. Ein Fahrerlebnis, das nur offene Automobile vermitteln können.
Der Alfa Romeo Spider wurde von Pininfarina entworfen und ist eine gelungene Mischung aus Ästhetik und Funktionalität. Das Abrißheck trägt wesentlich zur besseren Aerodynamik und zur hervorragenden Straßenlage bei.
Der Komfort dieses Wagens steht seinen Fahrleistungen in nichts nach. Vor allem verdient natürlich seine Fahrstabilität sowohl auf geraden Strecken als auch in der Kurve Erwähnung. Dazu kommt die Position und Form der Sitze, die auch bei längeren Reisen ein entspanntes und angenehmes Fahren ermöglichen. Sie passen sich dem Körper optimal an und weisen eine anatomisch körpergerechte Formgebung auf. Sie sind längs und in der Neigung verstellbar und garantieren eine ideale Lenkposition. Beide Sitze sind mit verstellbaren Nackenstützen ausgestattet.

The Spider offers you a completely new and pleasant sensation: direct contact with nature, sun and wind. A experience that only open cars can offer.

The Alfa Romeo Spyder was designed by Pininfarina an successful blend of esthetics and functionality. The cut contributes significantly to better aerodynamics and superb holding.

The comfort of this car does not rank below its performance. Ab its stability, whether on straight roads or curves, deserves ment do the position and form of the seats, that make possible a relaxi pleasant ride even on long trips. They fit the body optimally an an anatomically correct form. They are adjustable in length a and guarantee an ideal driving position. Both seats are fitte adjustable headrests.

Left: Now they spoke of an opening rear and its aerodynamic advantages. The name Pininfarina comes up again too.

Right: The Spider top was in fact as easy to operate as it looks here. But the car did look better open than with top up—like almost all convertibles. A hardtop was also still available.

Die Innenausstattung wird den Ansprüchen gerecht, die man an einen Luxuswagen und an ein Karosseriedesign der Spitzenklasse stellt. Besonders elegant wirkt die Formgebung des Armaturenbrettes und des Lenkrades. Der Kofferraum ist groß genug, um das Gepäck aufzunehmen, auf das ein Cabriolet-Fahrer normalerweise verzichten muß.

The interior furnishings meet the demands that one places on a luxury car and a top-rank body design. The shape of the dashboard and the steering wheel are particularly elegant. The luggage space is big enough to hold the luggage that a convertible driver must normally do without.

Alfa Romeo fans are sporting young people, these photos suggest to the observer. The photos come from a colorful brochure whose title page is reproduced on page 49. The somewhat problematic seat-belt anchoring is not visible in these pictures.

Right: fully opened, the brochure continued with these appealing pictures, extending to a breadth of almost 87 centimeters.

1980

Spider Alfa Romeo.

It is beyond doubt that the Two-liter was a speedy car: from zero to 100 kph in 11 seconds!

Fahrleistungen
Im folgenden die wichtigsten Daten des Alfa Romeo Spider:

2000 cm³-Motor:
- Leistung 93 kW (127 DIN PS)
- Höchstgeschwindigkeit: über 190 km/h
- 1 km aus dem stehenden Start in 30,8 sec.

Beschleunigung
Bei nur 4200 min⁻¹ bringt der Spider 2000 bereits seine volle Leistung: ein maximales Drehmoment von 180 Nm (18,4 kgm). Diese Zahl sagt alles aus über die Spurtkraft des Spider, der an der Ampel als Erster davonzieht und den Verkehr „abschüttelt".
Es reicht jedoch die Hälfte der Leistung aus, um eine Geschwindigkeit von 140 km/h zu halten. Die andere Hälfte steht jederzeit als Leistungsreserve zur Verfügung, um in heiklen Fahrsituationen sofort eingesetzt zu werden.

Performance
Here follow the most important data for the Alfa Romeo Spider:
2000 cc motor:
- Power 93 kW (127 DIN HP)
- Top speed over 190 kph
- 1 km from a standing start in 30.8 seconds

Acceleration
At only 4200 min-1, the spider already reaches its full power: a maximum torque of 180 Nm (18.4 kgm). This figure says everything about the quickness of the Spider, which is the first to pull away from the traffic light and "shake off" the traffic.

But even half of this power is ample to hold a speed of 140 kph. The other half is always at your disposal as a power reserve, to be applied at once in critical situations.

Healthy world,
healthy environment.
Who wouldn't want
to swap his sedan for
a convertible here . . .

The Motor
The 2000 cc motor of the Spider stands out through its very high torque and horsepower, which are achieved by the typical Alfa Romeo construction concept:

- The hemispherical combustion chambers allow a maximum thermodynamic and volumetric degree of motor functioning.
- The overhead valves with two camshafts guarantee the highest precision of activation and continual use.
- The intake and exhaust lines are designed so that they guarantee optimal filling of the cylinders with fuel.
- Natrium-cooled exhaust valves, as developed for aircraft motors, keep their own temperature low and are therefore resistant to heat tension.
- Two double carburetors, adjusted for optimal fuel supply, thus assure the lowest possible fuel consumption at all speeds.
- The fifth gear is another Alfa Romeo plus, since it is no mere auxiliary gear, thus not "overdrive". The five-speed gearbox contributes essentially to the robustness of the motor and its economical fuel consumption. not only at high speed on the superhighway but also under the most varied driving conditions. But above all, it promotes driving pleasure, supporting the motor's peppiness and acceleration even at high speeds.

A further aspect of the typical Alfa Romeo relationship between performance and safety is the Spider's body structure:

The weight distribution is excellent and contributes to optimal driving stability, just as the aerodynamic styling does.
- The Spider is equipped with 165 HR 14 tires, which are suited to high performance. The roadholding is optimal because of the classic rear axle with its torsion stabilizer.
- The brake system consists of two independent brake circuits. The dual-circuit system works independently on the front and rear wheels. The main brake cylinder with built-in pressure servo brake consists of two separate pump elements on one axis, by which the brake circuits are controlled independently of each other. The rear circuit includes a braking-power regulator, which equalizes the braking effect on the front and rear axles depending on brake-pedal pressure and prevents the rear wheels from locking. The large-dimension brake discs and the effective ventilation prevent a decrease in braking effect resulting from the heat of long and hard braking. This braking system gives the following important advantages: greatest functioning safety, less pedal pressure, high delay values.
- The body has been developed so that the passenger compartment is protected by progressively acting deformable zones.

Der Motor

Der 2000 cm³-Motor des Spider zeichnet sich durch sehr hohe Drehmomente und Leistung aus, die durch das für Alfa Romeo typische Konstruktions-Konzept erzielt werden:

- Die halbkugelförmigen Verbrennungsräume ermöglichen einen maximalen thermodynamischen und volumetrischen Wirkungsgrad des Motors.
- Die obenliegenden Ventile mit zwei Nockenwellen garantieren höchste Steuerungspräzision und Betriebskontinuität.
- Die Einlaß- und Auslaßkanäle sind so ausgelegt, daß sie eine optimale Gemischfüllung der Zylinder gewährleisten.
- Natriumgekühlte Auslaßventile, wie sie für Flugmotoren entwickelt wurden, halten die Eigentemperatur niedrig und sind daher wärmespannungsresistent.
- Zwei Doppelvergaser, die so eingestellt sind, daß sie optimale Kraftstoffzufuhr und damit geringstmöglichen Kraftstoffverbrauch in allen Fahrbereichen sicherstellen.
- Der fünfte Gang ist ein weiteres Alfa Romeo-Plus, da er kein zusätzlicher Gang, also kein „overdrive", ist. Das Fünfganggetriebe trägt wesentlich zur Robustheit des Motors und zur Wirtschaftlichkeit im Verbrauch, nicht nur bei hoher Geschwindigkeit auf der Autobahn, sondern auch unter den verschiedensten Fahrbedingungen, bei. Vor allem aber fördert es das Fahrvergnügen, da es die Spurtfreudigkeit und das Beschleunigungsvermögen des Motors im oberen Geschwindigkeitsbereich noch unterstützt.

Ein weiterer Aspekt des für Alfa Romeo typischen Leistung/Sicherheits-Verhältnisses ist die Karosseriestruktur des Spider:

- Die Gewichtsverteilung ist hervorragend und trägt ebenso wie die aerodynamische Linienführung zu einer optimalen Fahrstabilität bei.
- Der Spider ist mit 165 HR 14-Reifen bestückt, die sich für hohe Fahrleistungen eignen. Die Bodenhaftung ist aufgrund der klassischen Hinterachse mit Torsionsstabilisator optimal.
- Das Bremssystem besteht aus zwei voneinander unabhängigen Bremskreisen. Die Zweikreisbremse wirkt getrennt auf die Vorder- und Hinterräder. Der Hauptbremszylinder mit eingebauter Unterdruck-Servobremse besteht aus zwei verschiedenen, gleichachsigen Pumpenelementen, von welchen die beiden Bremskreise unabhängig voneinander gesteuert werden. Der hintere Bremskreis besitzt einen Bremskraftregler, der die Bremswirkung auf die Vorder- und Hinterachse abhängig vom Bremspedaldruck ausgleicht und das Blockieren der Hinterräder verhindert. Die großzügig dimensionierten Bremsscheiben sowie die wirksame Belüftung verhindern ein Nachlassen der Bremswirkung infolge der bei langen und heftigen Bremsgängen entstehenden Hitze. Dieses Bremssystem weist folgende wichtigen Vorteile auf: Höchste Betriebssicherheit, geringer Bremspedaldruck, hohe Verzögerungswerte.
- Die Karosserie ist so entwickelt worden, daß die Fahrgastzelle vorne und hinten durch progressiv wirkende Knautschzonen geschützt wird.

Text and picture may not fit together perfectly, but here they are in a 1980 Spider brochure. That the fifth gear is "not overdrive" is a purely academic interpretation. Its ratio was 0.79 to 1!

56

Right: Greetings from old friends: the instrument panel of the 2000 Spider has scarcely changed at all.

The Dashboard
It includes all instruments that have always been regarded by Alfa Romeo as absolutely necessary for constant control of the most important operating elements of the vehicle: tachometer, oil-pressure gauge, water-temperature gauge, as well as the other instruments and indicator lights (speedometer, overall and daily odometers, etc.)

The operating elements are also characterized by Alfa Romeo style. Whoever has built fast and safe cars knows the importance of a practical arrangement of every lever, switch and control. The furnishing of the interior is completed with practical places to put road maps and other articles, as well as by a locking glove compartment and an ashtray with cigarette lighter.

Das Armaturenbrett

Es enthält alle von Alfa Romeo schon immer als unbedingt erforderlich erachteten Instrumente zur ständigen Kontrolle der wichtigsten Bedienungselemente des Fahrzeuges: Drehzahlmesser, Öldruckmesser, Wassertherm ometer; dazu kommen noch die übrigen Instrumente und Kontrolleuchten (Tachometer, Gesamt- und Tageskilometerzähler etc.).
Auch die Bedienungselemente sind vom Alfa-Romeo-Stil geprägt. Wer immer schnelle und sichere Wagen gebaut hat, weiß um die Bedeutung einer bedienungsgerechten Anordnung jedes Hebels, Schalters und Bedienungselementes. Die Ausstattung des Innenraumes wird durch praktische Ablagen und Fächer zur Unterbringung von Straßenkarten und anderen Gegenständen sowie durch ein abschließbares Handschuhfach und einen Aschenbecher mit Zigarettenanzünder vervollständigt.

1980

The last photo from the 1980 Spider brochure. The technical data could have been more complete, but the choice of ball-joint or rack-and-pinion steering was still available.

Technische Daten	Spider 2000
Zylinder	4 in Reihe
Bohrung mm	84
Hub mm	88,5
Zylinderinhalt cm^3	1948
Leistung kW (DIN PS) min^{-1}	93 (127)/5300
Drehmoment mkg DIN/min^{-1}	18,4/4200
Radstand mm	2250
Spurbreite vorn mm	1324
Spurbreite hinten mm	1274
Max. Länge mm	4120
Max. Breite mm	1630
Max. Höhe mm	1290
Leergewicht kg	1040
Höchstgeschwindigkeit	über 190 km/h
1 km aus dem stehenden Start sec.	30,8
Reifen	165 HR 14
Sitzplätze	2
Elektrische Anlage	12 Volt
Tankinhalt	51 Liter

Kraftstoffzufuhr: Zwei Doppelhorizontalvergaser.

Ventilsteuerung: Die hängenden, V-förmig angeordneten Ventile werden von zwei Nockenwellen über dazwischenliegende, im Ölbad gelagerte Ventilbecher gesteuert; natriumgekühlte Auslaßventile.

Elektrische Anlage: 540 W-Drehstromlichtmaschine.

Kupplung: Einscheibentrockenkupplung mit Torsionsdämpfer; progressive Wirkung; Membranfeder; hydraulische Betätigung.

Getriebe: Fünf synchronisierte Vorwärtsgänge und Rückwärtsgang; Knüppelschaltung.

Vorderradaufhängung: Einzelradaufhängung an Doppelquerlenkern; Schraubenfedern und hydraulische Teleskopstoßdämpfer; querliegender Torsionsstabilisator.

Hinterradaufhängung: Schraubenfedern und koaxial dazu angeordnete Teleskopstoßdämpfer; querliegender Torsionsstabilisator.

Hinterachse: An der tragenden Karosserie durch zwei Längslenker mit Gummipuffern befestigt; seitliche Verankerung durch Reaktionsdreieck, das am Rahmen und an der Hinterachse auf Gummipuffer gelagert ist.

Differential: Hypoidverzahnt.

Lenkung: Kugelumlauflenkung oder Schnecke und Rolle.

Bremsen: Scheibenbremsen auf allen vier Rädern; Zweikreis-Bremssystem mit Bremskraftregler, der abhängig vom Bremspedaldruck auf die Hinterräder wirkt; Unterdruck-Servobremse; vom Hauptbremssystem unabhängige Handbremse, die an entsprechende Bremstrommeln an den Hinterrädern wirkt.

Metalliclackierung und Leder-Polsterung sind Sonderausstattungen gegen Mehrpreis.

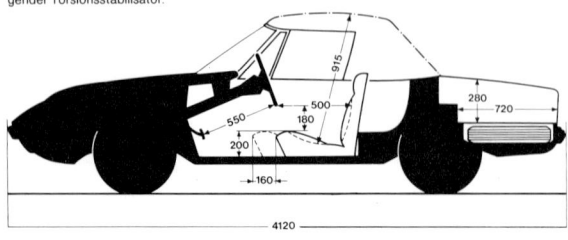

Daten, Beschreibungen und Illustrationen haben lediglich informativen Wert. Die Produkte können unterschiedliche Eigenschaften aufweisen, auch infolge konstruktiver Erfordernisse. Einige der im Prospekt beschriebenen und abgebildeten Ausstattungen sind nicht serienmäßig. Genaue Informationen erhalten Sie von Ihrem Alfa Romeo-Vertragshändler.
Grafiche Abidue - Sesto S. Giovanni 805 1080/3 D-CH-A

Technical Data Spider 2000
Cylinders 4 in-line
Bore in mm 84
Stroke in mm 88.5
Displacement in cc 1948
Power kW (DIN HP) min-1 93 (127)/5300
Torque mkg DIN/min-118.4/4200
Wheelbase in mm 2250
Front track in mm 1324
Rear track in mm 1274
Overall length in mm 4120
Overall width in mm 1630
Overall height in mm 1290
Dry weight in kg 1040
Top speed over 190 kph
1 km from standing start 30.8 seconds
Tires 165 HR 14
Seats 2
Electric system 12 volt
Fuel capacity 51 liters

Fuel supply: Two double horizontal carburetors.

Valve operation: The dropped V-form valves are activated by two camshafts via intermediate valve cups in an oil bath; natrium-cooled exhaust valves.

Electric system: 540-watt direct current generator.

Clutch: One-plate dry clutch with torsion damper, progressive action. Membrane spring, hydraulic activation.

Gearbox: Five synchronized forward speeds and reverse; stick shift.

Front suspension: Independent suspension with double transverse links, coil springs and hydraulic telescopic shock absorbers, transverse torsion stabilizer.

Rear suspension: Coil springs and coaxially located telescopic shock absorbers, transverse torsion stabilizer.

Rear axle: Attached to the body by two longitudinal links with rubber buffers; laterally anchored by reaction triangle mounted to the frame and rear axle on rubber buffers.

Differential: Hypoid gearing.

Steering: Ball-joint or rack-and-pinion.

Brakes: Disc brakes on all four wheels, dual-circuit system with braking-power regulator working on the rear wheels according to brake-pedal pressure, pressure servo brake, hand brake independent of the main braking system, working on brake drums on the rear wheels.

Metallic paint and leather upholstery are special features at additional prices.

Data, descriptions and illustrations have only an informative value. The products can have different qualities, including those resulting from construction requirements.

Some of the fittings described and depicted in the brochure are not production equipment. Exact information is available from your Alfa Romeo dealer.

58

Advertisement for the Alfa Romeo Spider 2000 Veloce made in USA. Composite photo from a brochure distributed by the importer in Englewood Cliffs, New Jersey.

1984

Left: Studio photo—completely to American taste. At right the colorful title page of this brochure—with a series of colorful variations of the traditional trade mark.

SPIDER VELOCE

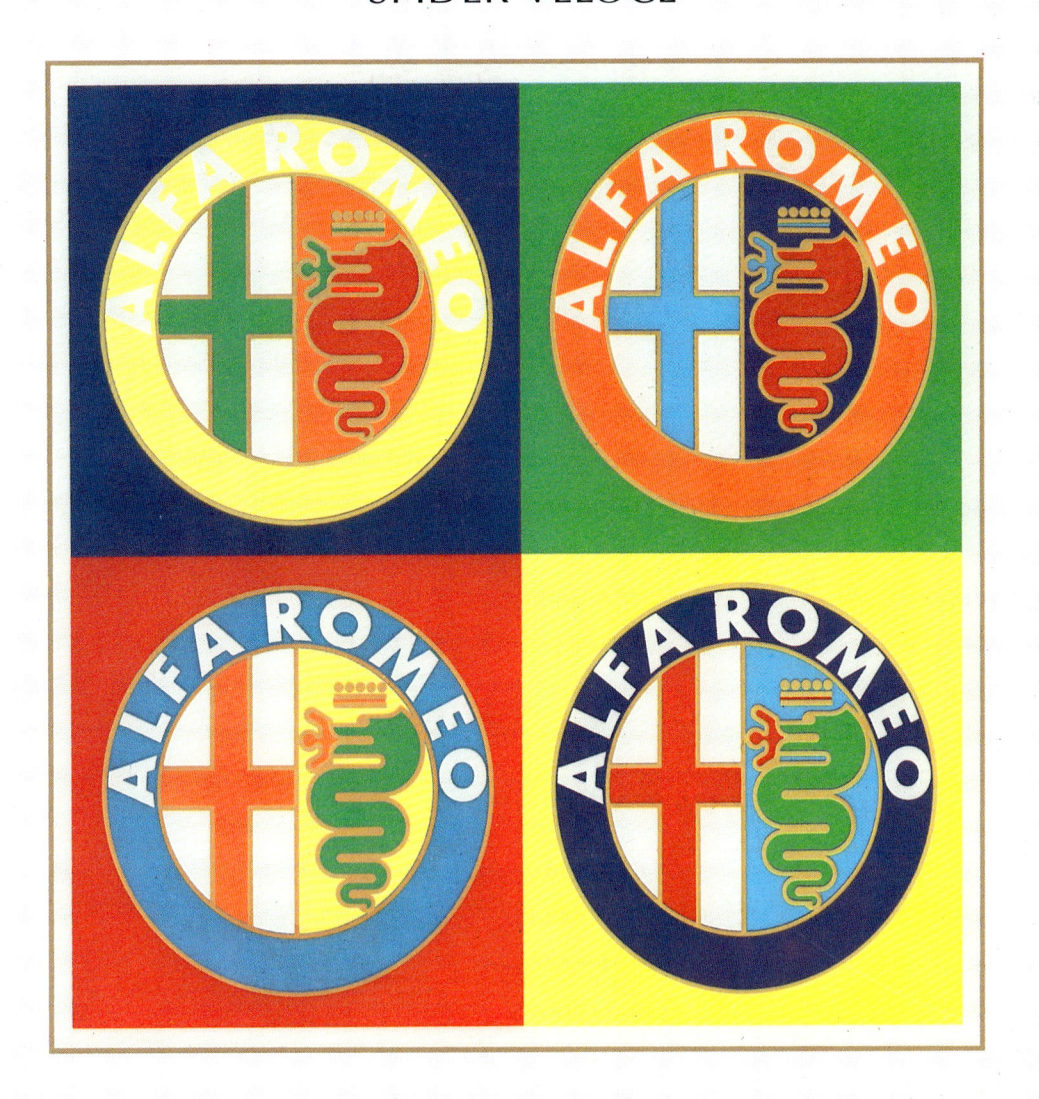

1984

Left: What Mary Miller in Milwaukee dreams of! "Let yourself be torn away by the spirit of the Alfa. At your nearest Alfa Romeo dealer!" it says in the brochure.

Right: Everything in matt black—even the last decorative chrome rings around the instruments (see page 57) have now disappeared. And there are a few more push-buttons.

Right: Here again the picture-pretty double-overhead-camshaft motor is shown. L-Jetronic fuel injection was long taken for granted for the entire USA, as well as Bosch electronic ignition.

62

1984

The illustrations on the
following pages are also from the
USA catalog shown here.

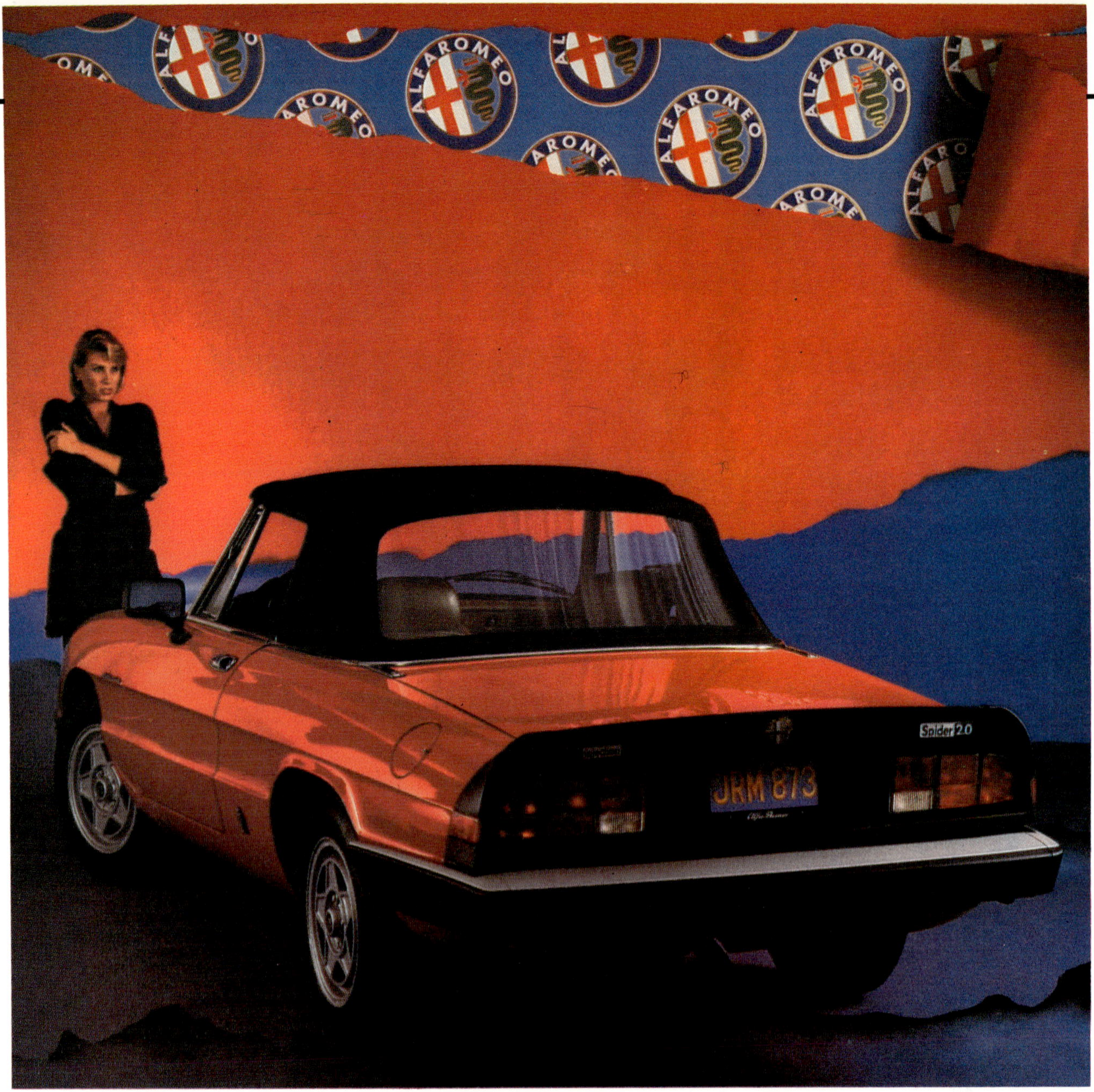
ALFA ROMEO
Spider 2.0
JRM 873

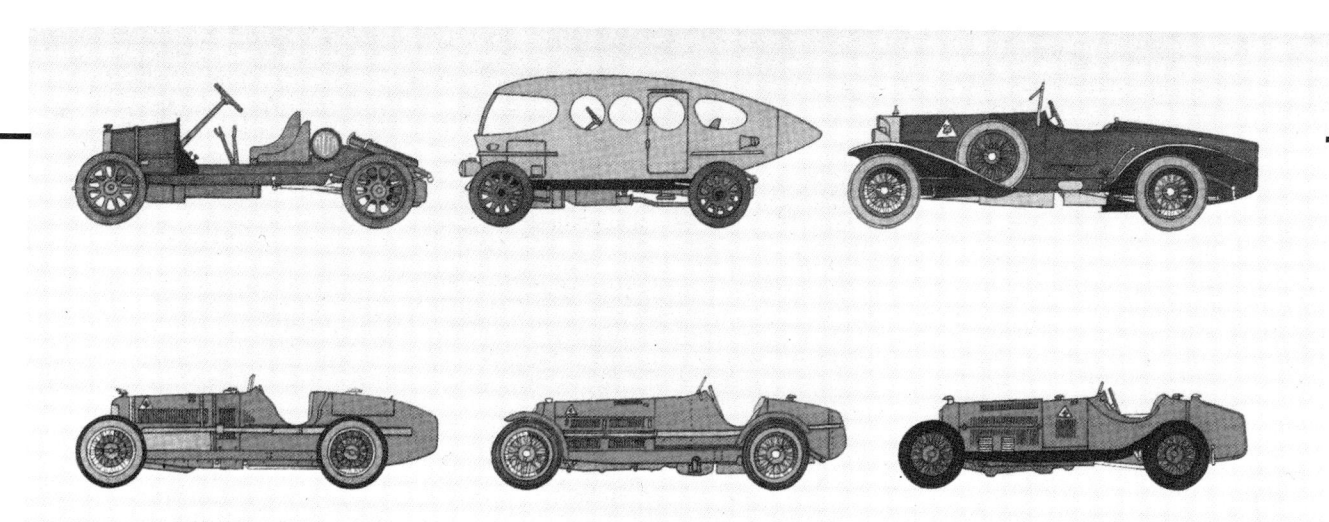

Some of Alfa Romeo's more noteworthy production and racing automobiles. From top left.

15-20 HP Series C (1910-1915); 40-60 HP Siluro (1914);
RL Supersport (1923); P2 (1924-1930); 8C 2300 Monza (1931);
P3 (1932); 8C 2900 (1938); Tipo 512 (1940); 159 (1950-1951);
33 TT 12 (1975); 182 (1982).

(On facing page) 6C 1750 (1929-1933).

1984

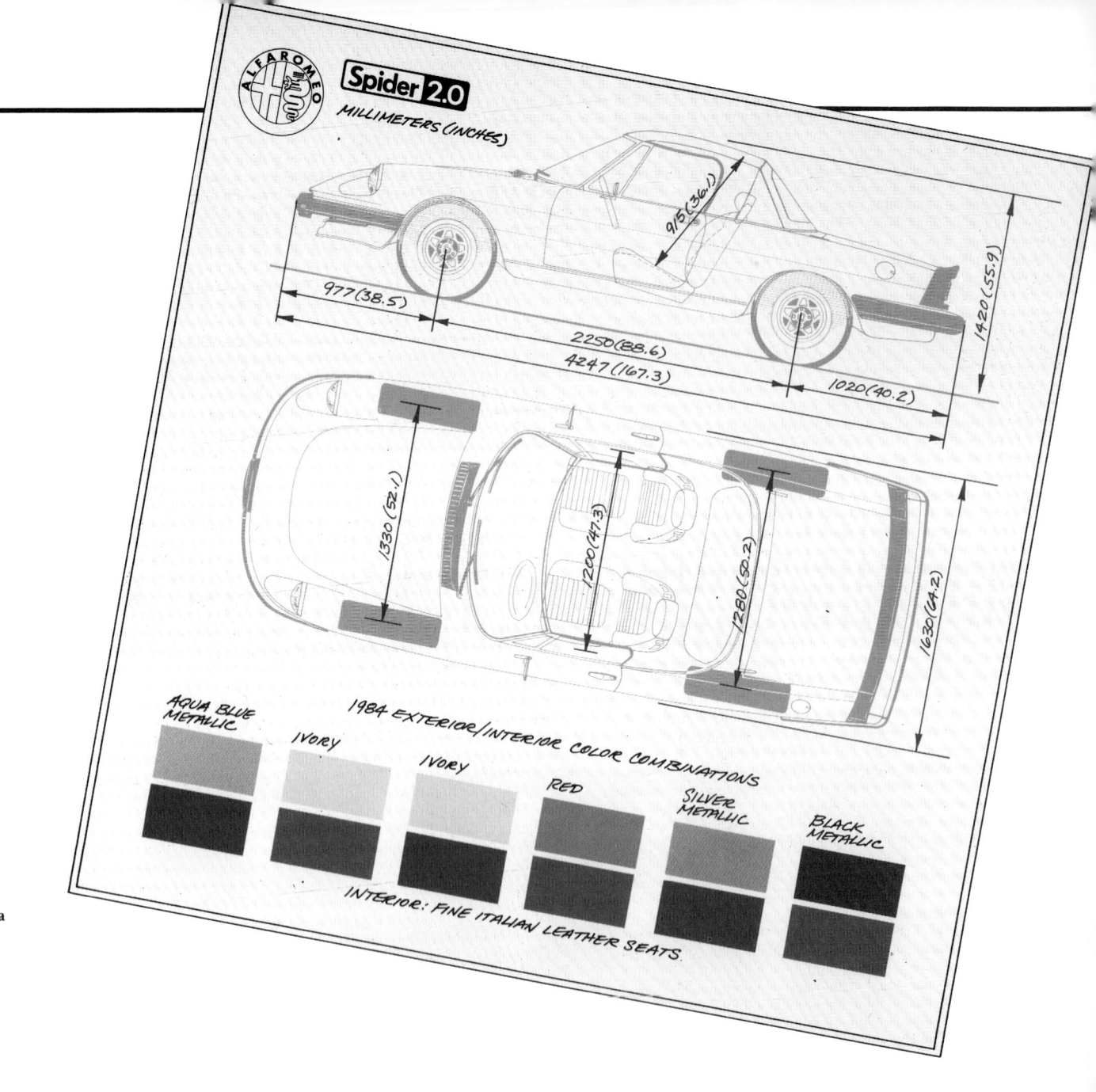

The US export version also had a factory-made leather interior. One had a choice of five color schemes. All it lacked was an automatic transmission.

1985

The Spider: Fresh-air Classic.

A new graphic line:
1985 Spider catalog.

Der Spider: Freiluft-Klassiker.

Alfa Romeo

1985

The Spider appeared forever young and fresh, especially in the advertisements. But these images corresponded completely to reality. With their open two-seaters, the Alfa firm always spoke to a young public, who (even when it could afford expensive cars) regarded neither the E-type nor the Corvette as an alternative. Spider customers often enough remained loyal to the brand.

Here is another all-out genre picture. The observer feels transported to the situation of the fresh, happy Alfa driver—one would like to be here too! The black bumpers and spoiler corners on the rear could almost be forgotten . . .

The Spider is accepted as a classic convertible. Its philosophy is enjoyment of individual movement far away from the uniformity of sedans: the fascination of open-air driving.

No automobile can transmit pure sportiness, vital driving enjoyment and the feeling of true freedom more directly than a convertible. The Alfa Romeo Spider is made for all those who seek a driving experience that has become rare: the direct contact with wind and sun, beyond all limitations. Fresh, free and fast.

Der Spider versteht sich als Cabrio-Klassiker. Seine Philosophie ist das Vergnügen an der individuellen Bewegung fernab jeder Limousinen-Uniformität: Die Faszination am Offen-Fahren.

Kein Automobil kann pure Sportlichkeit, vitalen Fahrspaß und das Gefühl wahrer Freiheit direkter vermitteln als ein Cabrio. Der Spider von Alfa Romeo ist für alle die geschaffen, die ein seltengewordenes Fahrerlebnis suchen: Den direkten Kontakt zu Wind und Sonne, jenseits jeder Enge. Frisch, frei und schnell.

Left: The dream world of the Eighties! This well-designed brochure was, for a change, produced in Germany.

69

Konsequente Linienführung prägt den neuen Spider von Alfa Romeo. Sein modifiziertes Design macht ihn unverwechselbarer denn je: Ein tief heruntergezogener Frontspoiler und ein auf die Abschlußkante des Kofferraums gesetzter Heckspoiler optimieren die Aerodynamik.

Sie passen sich formschön an das Gesamtdesign an und verbessern Fahrstabilität und Straßenlage.

Die neugestalteten Stoßfänger reichen jeweils bis zu den Radkästen.

Consequent design by Pininfarina.
The radiator grille had become a shaped piece without chrome decoration, with an Alfa Romeo emblem well placed in it.

Consequent designing characterizes the new Spider by Alfa Romeo. Its modified design makes it more unmistakable than ever: a front spoiler drawn deep down and a rear spoiler mounted on the rear edge of the trunk make for optimal aerodynamics.

They blend beautifully into the whole design and improve driving stability and roadholding.

The newly designed bumpers all reach to the wheel wells.

1985

The Enjoyment of Freedom

Der Spaß an der Freiheit.

Italian beach idyll. Good for sales material—but the car and the people in it feel better on a paved road.

Real open sports cars have become rare. The Spider by Alfa Romeo surely is one of the last originals of this classic genre of cars. And driving the Spider belongs all the more to an individual kind of automotive travel. The unbroken view of the sky, the wind blowing past your nose... This feeling makes driving the Spyder such a fascinating pleasure. And makes sedan drivers so envious.

Die echten, offenen Sportwagen sind rar geworden. Der Spider von Alfa Romeo gehört sicherlich zu den letzten Originalen dieser klassischen Automobil-Gattung. Und umso mehr gehört das Spider-Fahren zur individuellen Art automobiler Fortbewegung. Der ungetrübte Blick in den Himmel, der Fahrtwind um die Nase... Dieses Gefühl macht das Spider-Fahrvergnügen so reizvoll. Und Limousinen-Fahrer so neidisch.

Right: 18.1 mkp torque, 127 HP (or 93 kW)—and a nice typographical error in the technical data: 1360 kg top speed (instead of weight).

Vitality and mobility are typical of the Spider. Top speeds of over 190 kph (2.0 model) document its exclusive potential for performance. Then too, its extraordinarily favorable power-to-weight ratio makes for powerful acceleration. A five-speed gearbox supports the elasticity of the motor, allows a sporty driving style and contributes to economical fuel consumption.

Vitalität und Beweglichkeit prägen den Spider. Höchstgeschwindigkeiten von über 190 km/h (2.0 - Modell) dokumentieren sein souveränes Leistungsangebot. Dazu ermöglicht sein außerordentlich günstiges Leistungsgewicht eine kraftvolle Beschleunigung. Ein 5-Ganggetriebe unterstützt die Elastizität des Motors, erlaubt sportliche Fahrweise und trägt zur Wirtschaftlichkeit im Verbrauch bei.

1985

The excitingly new original.

Das aufregend neue Original.

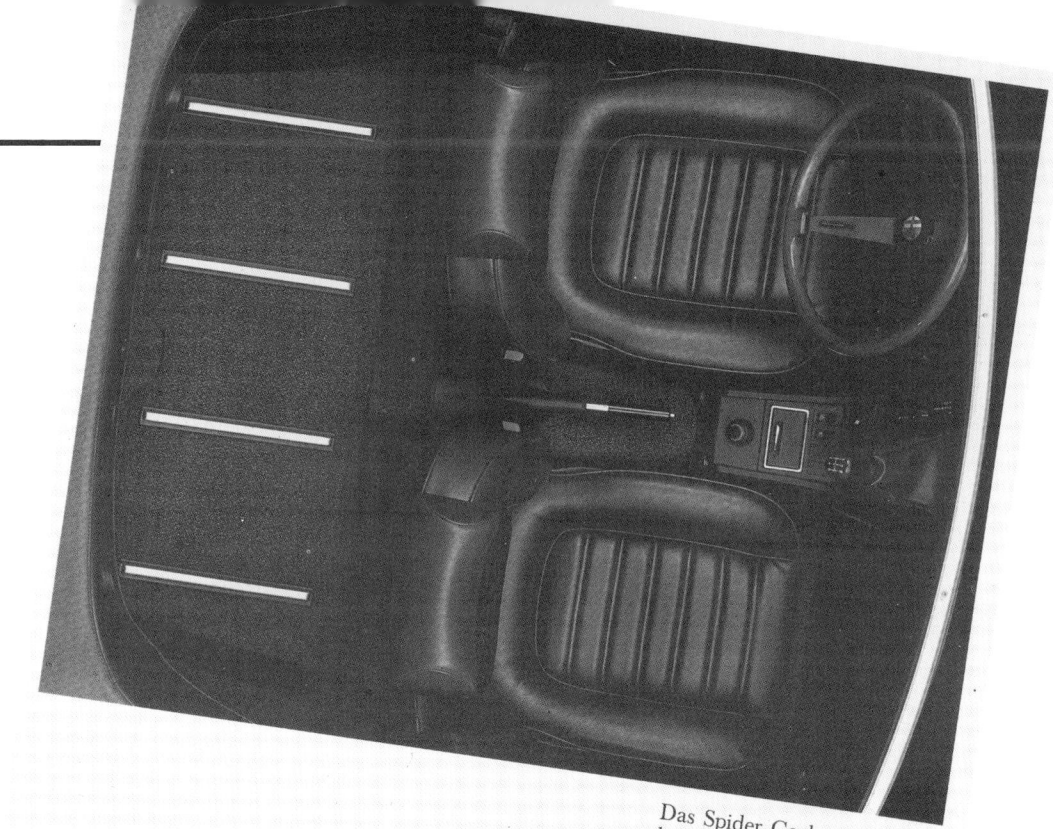

Left: Interior of the 1985 Spider. It is not a 2 +2, for one can put all sorts of extra luggage, shopping bags or a dog behind the seats.
The seat cushions have changed somewhat over the years. Pininfarina is still responsible for the design, inside and out.

Das Spider Cockpit vermittelt beste Cabrio-Tradition: Mit Holzlenkrad und einem neuen, funktional gestalteten Armaturenbrett mit klassischen Rundinstrumenten. Das voll versenkbare Verdeck läßt sich im Handumdrehen öffnen. Das Raumangebot ist reichlich bemessen:

The Spider cockpit expresses the best convertible tradition: with wooden steering wheel and a new, functionally designed dashboard of classic round instruments. The fully lowerable top can be raised with ease. The car offers plenty of space.

Der Spider präsentiert sich mit übersichtlicher und reichhaltiger Instrumentierung. Die Rundinstrumente und Kontrolleuchten sind übersichtlich und gut ablesbar angeordnet. Das funktionell gestaltete Armaturenbrett ist in Formgebung und Material so ausgeführt, daß Spiegelungen vermieden werden. Der Spider ist bestens gegen Regen und Schnee gewappnet: Mit einem einfachen Handgriff läßt sich sein Verdeck schließen. Eine wirksame Heizungs- und Belüftungsanlage mit zweistufigem Gebläse sorgt bei Kälte für einen behaglich temperierten Innenraum.

Die aerodynamische Linienführung des Spiders, für die der große Designer Pininfarina verantwortlich zeichnet, trägt wesentlich zur hervorragenden Fahrstabilität bei offenem sowie bei geschlossenem Verdeck bei.

The Spider presents visible and ample instrumentation. The round instruments and indicator lights are easy to see and situated to be read with ease. The functionally arranged instrument panel is executed in terms of form and material so that reflections are avoided. The Spider is well-armed against rain and snow: with a simple motion the top can be raised. An effective heating and ventilating system with two-stage fan maintains a cozy interior temperature in cold weather.

The aerodynamic lines of the Spider, for which the designer Pininfarina takes the responsibility, contributes much to the outstanding driving stability with top up or down.

Here too, everything is matt black! Under the shift lever are the digital clock and the switch for the blinker system.

1 Drehzahlmesser
2 Tachometer
3 Blinker
4 Zündung
5 Kraftstoffanzeiger
6 Öldruckanzeiger
7 Temperaturanzeiger für Kühlwasser
8 Kontrolleuchte
 A Bremsbeläge
 B Handbremse
 C Choke
 D Ölstand
 E Nebelscheinwerfer (an/aus)
 F Parkleuchte
9 Radiokonsole
10 Luftschlitze

1. Tachometer
2. Speedometer
3. Directional lights
4. Ignition
5. Fuel gauge
6. Oil-pressure gauge
7. Water temperature gauge
8. Indicator lights:
 A. Brakes
 B. Hand brake
 C. Choke
 D. Oil level
 E. Fog lights (on/off)
 F. Parking lights
9. Radio
10. Air vents

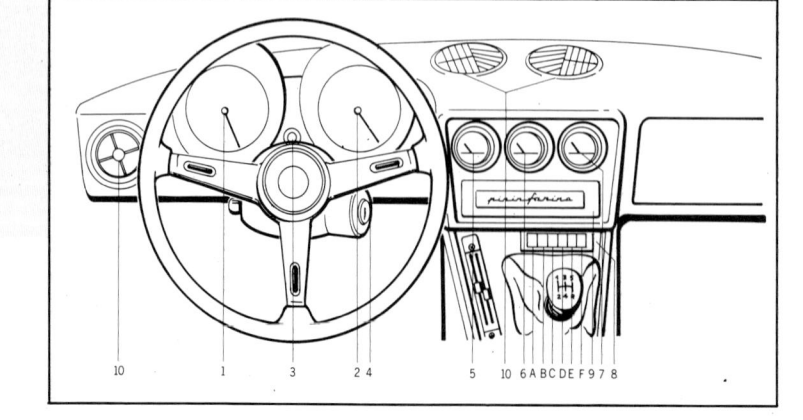

76

1986

Press photo of 1986, taken in Germany. The Spider has become a long-time classic!

Left: Title page of a four-page folded brochure of 1986. In three languages (Italian, French, German) the Spider is portrayed with special options and new hardtop.

Right: These wheels are also new. And through added profiling of the side panels, the vehicle takes on an interesting profile . . .

1986

ALFA ROMEO SPIDER

La Spider fa parte della natura. Si mimetizza col verde del paesaggio. Si confonde con i colori intorno. Si muove con la leggerezza del vento. Salire sulla Spider è sentirsi subito in viaggio verso mondi lontani. È fare parte di un ristretto club sportivo, di uno stile singolare, di un'atmosfera magica che ci avvolge non appena il vento scorre veloce ai lati della Spider. E poi l'arrivo, quel sottile senso di ammirazione che provoca la Spider ferma in attesa del suo pilota. Sono queste le emozioni che caratterizzano lo stile Spider. Con il nuovo elegante hard-top la Spider si trasforma in un moderno coupé pronto per affrontare anche le stagioni meno sorridenti dell'anno.

Le Spider se fond dans la nature. Il prend, comme par mimétisme, les couleurs des paysages qu'il traverse. Agile, il se déplace avec la légèreté du vent. Monter à bord d'un Spider, c'est se sentir partir vers des contrées lointaines; c'est être admis dans un club sportif fermé et élégant. C'est goûter à une atmosphère magique qui vous enveloppe dès que le vent caresse les flancs du Spider. A l'arrêt, tandis qu'il attend son propriétaire, c'est un murmure d'admiration qui l'entoure. Telles sont en résumè les émotions caractéristiques du style Spider. Le Spider se transforme avec le nouveau hard-top très élégant dans un coupé moderne et se prépare pour les saisons plus froides.

Der Spider versteht sich als Cabrio-Klassiker. Seine Philosophie ist das Vergnügen an der individuellen Bewegung fernab jeder Limousinen-Uniformität: Die Faszination am Offen-Fahren. Kein Automobil kann pure Sportlichkeit, vitalen Fahrspaß und das Gefühl wahrer Freiheit direkter vermitteln als ein Cabrio. Der Spider von Alfa Romeo ist für alle die geschaffen, die ein seltengewordenes Fahrerlebnis suchen: Den direkten Kontakt zu Wind und Sonne, jenseits jeder Enge. Frisch, frei und schnell. Mit dem neuen, eleganten Hard-Top wandelt sich der Spider in ein modernes Coupe, das auch die weniger angenehmen Jahreszeiten angenehm erscheinen läßt.

The added hardtop looks especially good on the Alfa Romeo Spider 2000. Naturally it is not included in series production, but can be bought extra. They speak of a convertible philosophy— and there certainly is one among Alfa enthusiasts.

The Spider is known as a classic convertible. Its philosophy is the enjoyment of individual movement far away from all the uniformity of sedan travel: the fascination of open-air driving. No automobile can deliver pure sportiness, vital driving fun and the feeling of true freedom, more directly than a convertible. The Alfa Romeo Spider is made for all those who seek a driving experience that has become rare: direct contact with wind and sun, without any limitation. Fresh, free and fast. With its elegant new hardtop the Spider turns into a modern coupe that makes even the less pleasant seasons of the year seem pleasant.

A Spider that could never be bought: an Alfa Romeo prototype built by Pininfarina in 1971, called the 33 Cuneo Stradale. The wedge shape of the body was a stylistic look forward into coming design directions (see the Triumph TR 7).

1986

Everything looks organized, matter-of-fact. But the small print points out: some of the equipment described in the brochure is not standard!

Displacement: 1962 cc
Maximum power: 128 HP at 5400 rpm
Maximum torque: 18.1 Kgm at 4000 rpm
Carburetion: 4 carburetors
Front & rear brakes: disc/disc
Top speed: + 190 kph
1 km from standing start: 30.8 seconds

Data, descriptions and illustrations have only an informative value. The products can have different characteristics, including those caused by construction requirements. Alfa Romeo reserves the right to make changes of all kinds in its products. Some of the equipment described in this brochure is not standard. See the price list.

			2.0/2.0 ✤
Cilindrata	Cylindrée	Hubraum	1962 cc
Potenza max	Puissance max	Maximalleistung	128 CV/5400 giri 1'
Coppia max	Couple max	Max Drehmoment	18.1 Kgm/4000 giri 1'
Alimentazione	Alimentation	Gemischaufbereitung	4 carb.
Freni ant/post	Freins av/arr	Bremsen vorn/hinten	Disco/Disco
Velocità max	Vitesse max	Höchstgeschwindigkeit	+ 190 Km/h
Km da fermo	Km départ arrêté	1 Km aus stehendem Start	30.8 s

Dati, descrizioni e illustrazioni hanno solo valore indicativo e i prodotti possono presentare caratteristiche diverse anche per esigenze costruttive. L'Alfa Romeo si riserva il diritto di qualsiasi modificazione ai suoi prodotti. Alcune delle dotazioni descritte e/o fotografate nell'opuscolo sono opzionali. Per il loro elenco completo vedere il listino prezzi.
Les renseignements fournis, descriptions et illustrations sont données à titre indicatif et les réalisations peuvent présenter des différences même pour des exigences de fabrication. Alfa Romeo se réserve à tout moment d'apporter des modifications aux véhicules de sa production. Parmi les accessoires mentionnés sur le dépliant certains sont optionnels. Voir liste complète sur le tarif prix.
Daten, Beschreibungen und Illustrationen haben lediglich informativen Wert. Die Produkte können unterschiedliche Eigenschaften aufweisen, auch infolge konstruktiver Erfordernisse. Alfa Romeo behält sich das Recht auf Änderungen aller Art an seinen Produkten vor. Einige der im Prospekt beschriebenen Ausstattungen sind nicht serienmäßig. Siehe dazu Preisliste.
Ediz. Ital./Franc./Ted. CH 862 201.

Alfa Romeo

Left: On the basis of the Alfa Romeo V6, Pininfarina presented this styling study of a Spider at the 1986 Geneva Salon (a coupe of this type was also to be seen). The lines fit into the design concepts, which were also realized by other auto manufacturers.

FOR SPORTING DRIVING

A brochure that was distributed in the spring of 1986. Here the "normal version" of the Spider can be seen again—without widened thresholds, special wheels or hardtop. The 1.6 and the 2.0 liter cars are both still offered.

SPIDER: THE OPEN INVITATION TO DRIVING FUN

Illustration: Spider 1600 Special metal-effect paint

(specification)	SPIDER 1600	SPIDER 2000
Cylinders	4 in-line	4 in-line
Displacement (cc)	1556	1948
Power (kW/HP)	76/103	93/127
Top speed (kph)	180	193
Length/width/height	4270/1630/1290	4270/1630/1290
Weight (kg)	1070	1070
Tires	165 HR 14	165/70 HR 14

The Spider belongs to the fresh-air classics that have become rare, made for the sort of motorists who value the enjoyment of individual mobility far away from the uniformity of sedans, and seek pure sportiness, agile driving fun and the feeling of true freedom. The fascination of open-air driving makes the Spider a convertible offer in the best Alfa Romeo tradition.

Technical Data: Alfa Romeo Spider 1955-86

Specification	Spezifikation		Giulietta Spider (Veloce)	2000 Spider	2600 Spider	Giulia Spider (Veloce)
Years Built	Baujahr		1955 (56)—62	1958—61	1962—65	1962 (64)—65
Wheelbase	Radstand	mm	2250	2500	2500	2250
Front Track	Spur vorne	mm	1292	1400	1400	1292
Rear Track	Spur hinten	mm	1270	1370	1370	1270
Dry Weight	Leergewicht	kg	860 (865)	1180	1220	885
Top Speed	Höchstgeschwindigkeit	km/h	165 (180)	175	200	172 (180)
Cylinders	Zylinderzahl		4	4	6	4
Bore	Bohrung	mm	74	84,5	83	78
Stroke	Hub	mm	75	88	79,6	82
Displacement	Zylinderinhalt	cm³	1290	1975	2584	1570
Horsepower at rpm	PS bei /min		80/6300 (90/6500)	115/5700	145/5900	92/6200 (112/...)
Tires	Zahl der Vorw.-Gänge		4	5	5	5
	Bereifung		155—15	165—400	165—400	155—15
Fuel Capacity	Tankinhalt	Liter	53	60	60	53
Number Made	Stückzahl		1430 (2796)	3443	2255	9250 (1091)

Specification	Spezifikation		Quattroruote Zagato Spider	1750 Spider Veloce	1300 Spider Junior	2000 Spider Veloce
Years Built	Baujahr		1966—68	1967—71	1968—72	1970—(86)
Wheelbase	Radstand	mm	2600	2250	2250	2250
Front Track	Spur vorne	mm	1290	1324	1324	1324
Rear Track	Spur hinten	mm	1270	1274	1274	1274
Dry Weight	Leergewicht	kg	750	1040	990	990
Top Speed	Höchstgeschwindigkeit	km/h	155	190	170	195
Cylinders	Zylinderzahl		4	4	4	4
Bore	Bohrung	mm	78	80	74	84
Stroke	Hub	mm	82	88,5	75	88,5
Displacement	Zylinderinhalt	cm³	1570	1779	1290	1962
Horsepower at rpm	PS bei /min		92/6000	118/5500	89/600	132/5500
Tires	Zahl der Vorw.-Gänge		5	5	5	5
	Bereifung		155—15	165HR—14	155SR—15	165HR—14
Fuel Capacity	Tankinhalt	Liter	66	46	46	51
Number Made	Stückzahl		92	8722	4538	

1600 Spider Duetto
1966—67
2250
1310
1270
990
185
4
78
82
1570
109/6000
5
155SR—15
46
6325

1600 Spider
1974—(86)
2250
1324
1274
990
185
4
78
82
1570
109/6000
5
165HR—15
51

Cutaway view of the 1570-cc displacement motor (Spider 1600), which produces 92 HP. The exhaust valves were natrium-cooled.

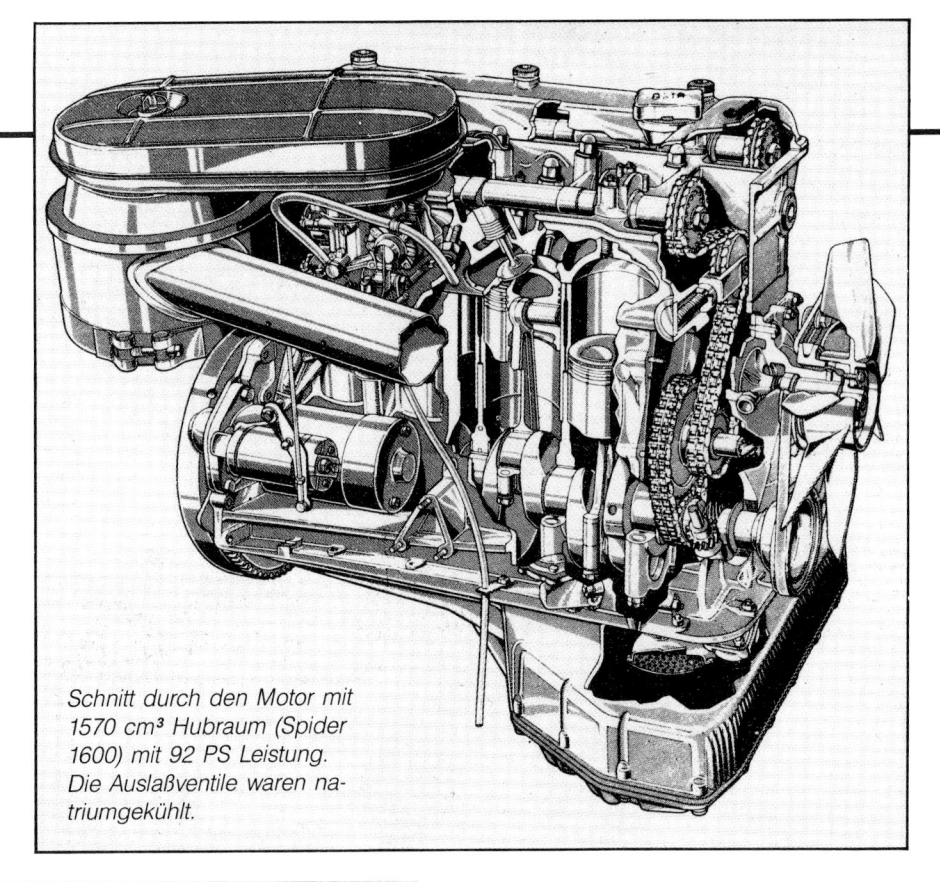

Schnitt durch den Motor mit 1570 cm³ Hubraum (Spider 1600) mit 92 PS Leistung. Die Auslaßventile waren natriumgekühlt.

Pininfarina tried building an Alfetta Spider in 1973. The two-seater with top bow, called the "Targa", did not go into production.

Alfa Romeo Spider in the Press

Alfa fans were spoiled—for years, by outstanding technology and aesthetic form. Whoever drove an Alfa, though, was also seen as an automotive outsider. Even today, this product is an exclusive brand. As a result, Alfa Romeo Spiders have seldom been reported on in the press.

In 1965 many looked forward to the new Spider with the rounded tail. Only later did sadness set in among the enthusiasts, who still later recalled the nostalgic rear styling of the Alfa convertible and found it more beautiful in hindsight. As a "spontaneous proof of appreciation" of how greatly the new bodywork was appreciated, is how *Auto, Motor und Sport* evaluated the thousand orders that were said to have been received when the new style was displayed (amounting to almost a third of the next year's production: 3300 of the cars were produced in 1967).

And yet: the round-tailed Spider 1600 was a successful creation. An eye-catcher, as the press confirmed: "Psychologists speak of the sex appeal of rounded forms that certainly can be found in a car body. After several weeks of test driving, we can confirm that Master Pininfarina did not miscalculate."

But more important were the new space and sight conditions: "Compared to its predecessor, the new Spider has grown: it is 35 cm longer, 7 cm wider and 4.5 cm lower, while the 2250 mm wheelbase remains unchanged. The long front and rear body overhangs—the Spider is 17 cm longer than the Sprint Coupe, though its wheelbase is 10 cm shorter—are regarded as "soft ends" that deform and absorb energy in an accident.

Additional centimeters are also found inside, where they are most welcome. In width particularly, one has more freedom of movement than in the earlier model. Then too, the spaces behind the seats were enlarged, so that small pieces of luggage could be stowed there even when the top is folded. But spare seats in back are not considered; the Alfa Spider

Face of the 1962/63 Giulia Spider model.

remains a true two-seater." Manfred Jantke, editor in Stuttgart, described the top of the Spider as a "two-man tent", but agreed that driver and passenger have enough headroom, since the seats are set deep enough. Only men measuring 1.85 meters or more had some problem with legroom—which was, of course, true of many Italian cars... But: "Although the window areas were enlarged and the sight conditions improved, two items are still not satisfactory: the upper rim of the windshield frame is

Above: Giulia GTC with hardtop, of 1965. Left: 2000 Spider Touring of 1958.

Right: Spider 1600 of 1980.

The way mechanism was built was a real joy, it was said further. In 15 seconds the top could be put up or down, without one's having to get out—even while in motion (by the passenger). It was particularly noted that the luggage space could be opened from the driver's seat and was also relatively large, since the spare wheel and fuel tank were located under the floor.

rather low for tall drivers and obscures their view of traffic lights. Even worse are the large dead areas formed by the top at the rear sides, making entry onto superhighways and priority roads difficult. Alfa Romeo ought to add additional corner windows to the top, as the English do to their roadsters. Otherwise the top is well made."

Not much appreciation was given to the plexiglas headlight covers (which were later done away with, as is well known). "According to the factory, they add 6 kph to the top speed"—but in warm, damp weather they tended to become misty on the inside, like those of the Matra and Alpine. "Dirty water splashed up by the wheels also obscures the light."

But all in all, only minor fault could be found with the Spider, such as the wind noise and limited view with the top up: characteristics shared with many

Left: 2600 Spider with body by Touring (Superleggera). Below: Driver's seat of the 1966 Spider Duetto.

Right: Cockpit of the 1962 Giulia Spider. There were as yet no seat belts here.

other roadsters and sports cars. The Alfa Romeo's advantages were stressed all the more: the motor's flexible performance and power, the good driving characteristics, the brakes (discs all around), the roominess of the car.

"Alfa's wonderful dohc motor has ranked for over ten years among the most progressive sport motors in the world", it was said (with a note that Alfa had been making dohc engines since 1928, and even then the powerplant was regarded as progressive). "For the Spider and the equally new GTV Coupe a new performance variation was developed: the 1600-cc Veloce motor with 109 DIN HP. Once again the Milanese specialists have developed new cam shapes and a new carburetor adjustment to improve performance and its characteristics.

"This time they held an especially hot hand: despite the increase in stated power, the polar moment was also improved considerably in the lower engine-speed range. In the Veloce motor it is over 14 mkg from 2500 to 5000 rpm, while the 106 HP motor (which is still used in the normal Sprint GT)

86

attains this figure only from 2800 to 3800 rpm. The requirement for such good power curves, which have been typical of Alfa Romeo engines since way back when, are created by the Milanese factory with two Weber double-throat carburetors, the potential of which is used to the fullest here."

The powerful acceleration of the new Veloce motor did much to define the character of the car, Jantke write. It is a strong sports car but not a

Spider 2600. Something for tough men!

nervous one. "One can let it drag along at 3000 rpm like an MGB or TR4 without having to accuse oneself of sloppy driving. From as low as 1500 rpm up, the car accelerates smoothly in fifth gear, which is really sensational for a 1600-cc motor with 109 HP. In the city one generally uses fourth gear with no more trouble than in an Opel Rekord. The most powerful Alfa motor (other than the GTA racing motor) is at the same time the smoothest and most pleasant."

The fact that one was really getting a lot of car for one's money was made clear by one point that the well-known motoring journalist made: "Since the departure of the Porsche 356, the choice of affordable open sports cars has not been at all great. Those who love to feel the wind blowing through their hair and know they are going fast will simply have to notice the Alfa Romeo. Where else does one find a dual-overhead-camshaft motor, a five-speed gearbox, four disc brakes, belted tires and a power-to-weight ratio below 10 kg/HP effectively united for 13,000 Marks? The Alfa, already known in the vulgate as "Osso di Sepia" (octopus cuttlebone) before a price announcement officially named it "Duetto", is a hit at the price."

13,000 Marks in 1966—even in the fall of 1958 the Spider Veloce had cost 16,900 Marks. "It is not cheap", said an Alfa advertisement, written at that time by the importing firm, NSU (!), "but reasonably priced, like a good watch or valuable diamond." In 1975 the Spider cost 15,990 Marks, a year later a thousand Marks more. The Spider 2000 reached 24,990 Marks by 1980—that was 2500 Marks more than a Triumph TR7 cost. The magazine *Sportfahrer* compared the Alfa two-liter with such a sports car; "Both belong to the ever-rarer breed of fresh-air cars that do not inhibit the occupants' feeling of freedom with a massive roll bar." In comparison with the Triumph's technology, the Alfa already seemed rather like an oldtimer. In 1970 the round-tailed Spider, born in Turin in 1965, was given a new body, "which improved its appearance yet weakened the body's stability". But then as before, the Alfa Spider enjoyed enthusiastic praise. "Its age is clear to see, but it still has charm." Even the unfortunate wheel size could not change that much, nor the plastic caps over the headlights, which were still present. "Why the Alfa Spider hides its thin 165 tires under its fenders while the other Alfas roll around on tires of the Seventies series" was scarcely comprehensible. In comparison to the Alfa, the steering of the TR7 was lighter, but in terms of the chassis, neither lost any ground to the other. With a speed of 192.2 kph, the Italian was also clearly faster than the Briton with its 174.7 kph. The latter also used more fuel: 11.4 liters of premium, compared to the Alfa's 10.8 liters for an average 100 kilometers. Both had five-speed gearboxes. "Alfa fans are nostalgic", said *Sportfahrer* editor Harald Prüsslmann; they won't drive anything but this Italian monument to convertibles, yet they wait longingly for a new version of their favorite to appear . . .

The Alfa Spider certainly did not look like an oldtimer to the car tester Fritz Reuter, who wrote in *Auto, Motor & Sport* in 1971: "The newest variant of this Spider scarcely leaves anything to wish for! The car ranks among the few open cars that can be driven almost at top speed with top down without undue disturbance from the wind. Thus open driving, even with rolled-down side windows, is a remarkable lot of fun even at high speeds!"

The object of his testing was the new 1750 with "fastback"—a style "that becomes the car very well—especially with the top down. This body change, long wished for by many Spider fans, not only is a plus optically but also has practical advantages." Reuter praises the increased luggage space (now able to hold 188 liters). But the round-tailed Spider was still available—because it sold well in the USA.

Other improvements listed by Reuter include:
* Dual-circuit brake system
* Hanging brake and clutch pedals
* New air filter
* New radiator grille
* New front and rear bumpers with rubber pads
* New front parking and directional lights, changed license platelight
* New indented door handles
* New dashboard design with instruments rearranged and central console
* Additional choke, brake fluid and hand-brake warning lights
* New seats with (optional) adjustable headrests, plus new rear seats.

The 1750 Spider's interior decor was also new. "The seats convince you by their body-oriented form and excellent side support; the occasional seats in the rear are more suited for use as extra luggage space

Left: view of the engine compartment of a 1962 Giulia Spider. The perfectly restored car is on display at the Ibbenbüren Automobile Museum.

than for holding passengers: only small children would have sufficient space in them, and then only when the front seats are moved far forward. So the Fastback Spider is not a genuine 2 + 2. But two people find plenty of space available—especially in terms of width. With one limitation: the legroom is somewhat short for very tall drivers, especially for the foot that goes on the gas pedal and can only relax when the pedal is all the way to the floor.

"As with all Alfa models, the interior is luxuriously and tastefully decorated. Two large round instruments, haded by visors, give information on engine and road speed; three smaller gauges located in the central console indicate fuel level, oil pressure and water temperature, and the tilted three-spoked wooden steering wheel looks especially nice in front of the matt black dashboard. The switches for windshield wipers, dashboard lighting and the two-speed electric fan are located under the shift lever, which grows out of the central console and, in true Alfa style, is set in a voluminous leather sack; they can be reached quickly there at any time—in fact, all operating controls are located where they are easy to see and use.

"The top of the open Alfa is also characterized by being easy to use, as this point shows: it can be raised or lowered in a few seconds without requiring the driver to get out—a very valuable advantage in our quickly changing weather conditions, which makes it possible to enjoy even the smallest sunbeam without lengthy fumbling. In addition, the closed top of the test car proved to be watertight and free of drafts, so that one felt well protected even in a bad storm. The sight conditions were less good with the top up; the low windshield hinders the view of traffic lights, and the big dead corners at the rear sides obscure the view in heavy traffic or when merging. Here an improvement suggested by *Auto, Motor & Sport* long before could provide help: Alfa ought to adopt the type of top used on the Fiat Dino Spider, also built by Pininfarina, in which the rear window is extended to the sides and can also be opened with a zipper. Along with a better view, this would also provide an additional, and quite fascinating, variation on the open-top theme."

Lack of stability has often been cited as an argument against open cars—not to mention the rattling that results from it. But such side effects will not spoil an Alfa driver's enjoyment of fresh-air motoring. "The test car neither developed disturbing sounds, nor did it show any great body flexing. This solidity of the body, along with the functional and easy-to-use interior, are the reasons why one feels very good in an Alfa after just a few kilometers."

One major reason for feeling good when driving the Alfa 1750 Spider is the powerplant, the tester wrote. The power train knows how to mobilize its 113 HP with impressive ease, and the enormous elasticity that lets the motor handle any driving situation with power and quickness is also noteworthy. One has the feeling that there are at least two and a half liters of engine displacement under the hood.

"From the very start the machine shows its best side: It always gets right to work willingly with the first turn of the ignition key, and it runs absolutely smoothly even in the first few meters. In the process, it enchants the enthusiast's ear with the healthy sound of its exhaust, which in the 1750 Spider—especially with the top down—sounds particularly full and sporting, so that one makes more use of the easily shifted five-speed gearbox, with its evenly spaced ratios, than is necessary in view of the engine characteristics: Between 2000 and 2500 rpm the auditory feast is at its richest, which is why one tries often enough to stay in that range as long as possible by shifting busily.

"The motor doesn't seem to care at what speed and in which gear one normally accelerates, for it has enough power to offer practically all the time. Even from 1500 rpm on it works willingly and powerfully. This praiseworthy behavior results in untroubled driving, which is particularly relaxing in today's heavy traffic. And if one—in passing, for example—really has to call on all the car's reserve power for acceleration, then the five gears, taken in order, provide greater superiority than the standing-start acceleration figures would lead one to expect."

In ten seconds the Spider tested by *Auto, Motor und Sport* accelerated from zero to 100 kph, and its top speed was 191.5 kph. Fuel consumption during the test amounted to 13.7 liters per 100 kilometers of driving. "Remarkably low", Reuter commented. Then he went on to speak of the suspension: "Thanks to the costly suspension of the rigid rear axle and the successful agreement of springing and damping, the Alfa Spider possesses superb handling conditions. Fast superhighway driving is just as problem-free for it as nimble handling of curves. The one is improved by good directional stability, the other by a very neutral handling that changes to a mild, always controllable oversteer only in the borderline area. On tighter curves one can bring on this oversteering by additional pressure on the gas pedal, though in the process the inner rear wheel tends to rotate."

Only on an extremely wavy surface or on a road with bad frost heave did the limits of the rigid rear axle make themselves felt. But the Alfa lost none of its good-naturedness even then. "Driving comfort also profits from the harmonious cooperation of the suspension. Because of the relatively short wheelbase and the very short distance of spring movement, of course, one cannot expect any extraordinary results, but the whole impression is thoroughly positive. In any case, the suspension is not to blame if one no longer feels fresh as the morning dew at the end of a long trip: There are—as in most convertibles—wind sounds that make themselves heard at high speeds. Above 140 kph they attain a volume that makes any conversation difficult and can have a fatiguing effect over the course of time."

Such problems—at least officially!—were not noticed by the Americans. In the USA, where a large part of the Alfa production has been sold from the start, the 55-mph limit has been in force for some time, as Mike Knepper wrote in the magazine *Car & Driver:* "A sports car, by an early definition, is supposed to be fast above all else. Let's forget that. A sports car is supposed to be fun." His comparison test appeared in April of 1979 with the subtitle "Just

Right: Rear view of the Spider 1600 with top up.

for Fun", and compared the Alfa Spider Veloce with five competitors: the Fiat Spider 2000, Corvette L-82, Datsun 280ZX, Mazda RX-7 with Wankel motor and Porsche 924. The Alfa was equipped with Spica fuel injection.

Naturally the Corvette, with its 5.8-liter V8 motor and more than 200 HP, was the fastest car, but that was not the testing criterion. In terms of roadholding the Alfa was "good to very good"—but disadvantages were also noted, at least in testing on a closed course at Willow Springs: "Fast downshifting is not the Alfa's strong point. Under heavy braking the rear end tends to break loose, just as the car rocks under abrupt deceleration. The Alfa and the Fiat resembled each other in that respect. They provide a lot of driving pleasure, but they should not be taken to the limits of their engine speeds on extreme courses." Of course, applying racing standards was scarcely the purpose of the comparison test. And it was precisely the Corvette that test driver Don Sherman rated best in driveability: "The limits of the big American could not be determined in this test." They tried to drive the Corvette to the limit till the tires smoked...

Smoking tires: it was just that which always impressed drag-racing fans who regard power and massiveness as the essence of sportiness. Those who have more awareness of cultivated car building (and driving) were more inclined to agree with Mr. Knepper when he wrote: "Alfa represents the old school. Cars of this brand are the finest embodiment of classic automobile construction that can be found today. These cars show the results of long years of research and experience. One might think that Alfa clung to qualities that had been exceeded—but in the end, the Italians stick to conclusions that have been accepted as right and have proved themselves." It is not surprising that the Porsche won the most points from the American test team. Then came the Wankel Mazda, and naturally the Corvette was in third place. Number four was the Alfa 2000 Spider. "Whatever one may think of sports cars," Knepper closed his report, "it is a matter of personal taste. If someone has never yet owned an Alfa Romeo, MG Midget or Triumph Spitfire, he will hardly be able to withstand the temptation to acquire such a car some day. But the technology of the Seventies has more to offer. It has made possible new sports cars that are faster, easier to handle, less tiring to drive..."

Cultivation and perfected construction or not—GM, Mazda and Porsche were certified as being more up-to-date. Yet year after year (in the USA too) a constant number of fans chose the "old-fashioned" Alfa Romeo Spider. In 1979 there were 3134 customers, in 1980 3743, in 1981 3132, in 1982 2864, in 1983 5142, in 1984 5850, in 1985 5237. The cheer of "Viva Alfa" seemed to grow no softer among convertible fans, overseas as well as in Europe. "A sports car is supposed to be fun", as Mike Knepper so correctly stated. The majority of other Americans have also left the flavor of smoking tires to their incorrigible power fans—at the wheel of a muscle car from Detroit.

In the summer of 1986 the press reported on negotiations on whose outcome the future of the Alfa Romeo firm depended. Whether Fiat or Ford would gain control was a question that remained open until late autumn (Excerpt from Automobile Revue, Bern).

Alfa-Rätselraten geht weiter

Von unserem ①-Mitarbeiter
Das Rätselraten um die Verhandlungen zwischen Alfa Romeo bzw. deren Finanzgruppe Finmeccanica einerseits und Ford anderseits geht weiter. Kaum hatte die italienische Presse angekündigt, dass alle Hindernisse beseitigt seien und die Unterzeichnung dicht bevorstehe, kam aus London die kalte Dusche in Form eines Dementis des Ford-Sprechers. Danach existierte keinerlei Geheimabkommen. Niemand könne sagen, wie lange noch verhandelt kommt, und das Problem der Schuldenübernahme durch die Amerikaner. Italienischerseits sträubt man sich entschieden gegen eine kurzfristige Zedierung des Kommandos an den Detroiter Riesen. Man möchte vielmehr diesen bitteren Verzicht auf die lange Bank schieben, gleichzeitig jedoch so bald wie möglich in den Genuss der Detroiter Geldpumpe kommen. Was die Verschuldung von Alfa Romeo betrifft, wird nach vorsichtigen Schätzungen das Ziel einer ausgeglichenen Jahresbi... von insgesamt 450 Milliarden Lire entstehen. Die noch ungelöste Streitfrage lautet: Ist Detroit bereit, die Hälfte davon, also 225 Milliarden, abzudecken?

Ungeklärt bleibt vorderhand auch noch, ob die Amerikaner bereit sein werden, die Forderung Alfa Romeos zu akzeptieren, wonach das Management von Arese und Pomigliano in italienischer Hand bleiben soll. Auf alle Fälle dürfte noch viel Zeit verstreichen, bis der Vertragsentwurf unterzeichnet wird

Alfa Guessing Game goes on *from our collabora*
The guessing game as to the negotiations between Alfa Romeo their financial group Finmeccanica on the one hand and Ford on other goes on. Scarcely had the Italian press announced that obstacles had been overcome and the signature was at hand, the cold shower came from London in the form of a denial from the F spokesman. According to that, there was no secret agreement. Nobo could say how long negotiations would continue and when communiqué on the subject could be expected.

There are still two controversial points: the question of at what ti Ford is to gain the absolute majority, and the problem of assum debts by the Americans. On the Italian side, the striving is definit against a short-term cession of command to the Detroit giant. O would rather move this bitter end far down the table while at the sa time enjoying the Detroit money pump as soon as possible. As for A Romeo's indebtedness, careful estimates place the goal of a balan yearly budget at not before 1990 (always assuming that the contr with Ford comes about and production can be increased significant Until then, though, losses will rise to a total of 450 billion Lira. T bone of contention, as yet unsolved, is: Is Detroit ready to cover hal that, 225 billion?

It is also not yet clear whether the Americans will be ready to acc Alfa Romeo's request that the management of the Arese a Pomigliano works remain in Italian hands. In any case, a lot m time is likely to pass until the contract is signed, and until Parliament in Rome says—if at all—yes and amen. *Klaus Rüh*

Alfa Romeo Spider in miniature

The number of Alfa Romeo models in scales from 1/8 to 1/87 is very great—they number in the hundreds. But only a few Spiders are among them, especially those after 1955 (Giulietta etc.). Here is a short list of these rarities, which cannot claim to be a complete one. And a number of these rare models are to be had today only at collectors' meets!

Alfa Romeo Giulietta Spider
Flyers (GB)	Readymade	Diecast	1/87
Impy (GB)	Readymade	Diecast	1/60
Buby-Solido (RA)	Readymade	Diecast	1/43
Brosol (BR)	Readymade	Plastic	1/43
Dalia-Solido (E)	Readymade	Plastic	1/43
EGM (I)	Readymade	Diecast	1/43
Metosul (P)	Readymade	Diecast	1/43 (2 types)
Sam Toys (I)	Readymade	Plastic	1/43
Solido (F)	Readymade	Diecast	1/43
Verem (F)	Readymade	Diecast	1/43
Politoys (I)	Readymade	Plastic	1/41
Paya (E)	Readymade	Metal/Plastic	1/32
Sam Toys (I)	Readymade	Plastic	1/23
Togi (I)	Readymade	Metal	1/20
Paya (E)	Readymade	Metal/Plastic	1/20

Giulia Spider
Togi (I)	Readymade	Metal	1/23

2000 Spider
Politoys (I)	Readymade	Plastic	1/41
Aurora (USA)	Kit	Plastic	1/32
Togi (I)	Readymade	Metal	1/23
Schuco (D)	Readymade	Metal	1/20 (2 types)

Duetto Spider
Mebetoys (I)	Readymade	Diecast	1/43 (2 types)
Novakit (I)	Kit	Plastic	1/43 (4 types)
Togi (I)	Kit	Metal	1/23

Zagato Spider 4 R
Politoys (I)	Readymade	Diecast	1/43

93

Literature for Alfa Romeo Fans

Alfa Romeo—Eight Decades of Italian Automobile Building by Hull, Slater & Schrader. This lavishly illustrated volume is the first German-language complete documentation of this great Italian make of automobile from 1910 to 1986, with a history of the firm, a complete listing of all types and racing victories. In a slipcase, 400 pp, 800 color and b/w illustrations.

Alfa Romeo—All Cars from 1910 by Luigi Fusi. One of the most thorough books on this make, with all models to 1976 and their technical data. 875 pp, 800 b/w illustrations, Italian/English text.

Alfa Romeo—Catalogue Raisonné by Luigi Fusi and Giovanni Lurani. Two massive volumes in one slipcase—the bible for all Alfa fans, covering all aspects of the firm's development and that of its cars. 550 pp, 1000 b/w and 24 color photos. Trilingual English/French/Italian text.

Alfa Romeo Great Marques by D. Owen. A colorful, interesting illustrated volume n the development of the Alfa marque. 80 pp, all in color, English text.

Illustrated Alfa Romeo Buyers Guide by Joe Benson. A guide to buying a collector car, with all historical, technical and practical information on the differences and development of the various models. Every model built to date is evaluated with a five-star system. 176 pp, 200 illustrations, English text.

Composizioni Alfa Romeo. A lavish color photo volume by Massimo Listri, with many detail shots. 104 pp, 104 color photos, Italian text.

Alfa immagini e percorsi edited by Angelo Tito Anselmi. This official catalog for an exhibition in Milan on the occasion of the firm's 75th anniversary includes photos and descriptions of all displayed cars and a history of the firm. 160 pp, 140 b/w photos and 32 color pages, Italian/English text.

L'Alfa Romeo—Grimaldi/Bandini/Lazzero/Gerosa. Four noted auto historians report on the 75-year history of the Alfa Romeo firm. 25 x 25 cm, 208 pp, 200 b/w photos, Italian text.

Zagato: From Alfa Romeo 1900 SSZ to TZ2 by Michele Marchiano. Another volume in this new series, dealing with Zagato models, this volume covers the Alfa Romeo types from the 1900 SSZ to the TZ2. All important data and many hitherto unpublished photos. 80 pp, approx. 80 illustrations in color and b/w, Italian/English text.

Alfa Romeo Giulietta by Angelo Tito Anselmi and Lorenzo Boscarelli. This volume in the Auto Classic Series includes all technical data, road-test reports, a short outline of the firm's history and a list of racing victories. 178 pp, very many color and b/w photos, Italian text.

Alfa Romeo Museum-Catalogue by Gian Cenzo. An up-to-date guide to the Alfa Museum in Arese. Tables list all models on display, with photos and technical data. 157 pp, 160 photos, some in color, Italian/English text.

Museo Alfa Romeo edited by the publishers of the Japanese magazine Car Styling. A complete listing of all museum vehicles with their technical data, augmented by illustrations covering the history of the marque. 175 pp, 300 b/w and 33 color photos, English/Japanese text.

Alfa Romeo Spiders by David Owen. This volume of the Auto History Series covers the famous Italian Spiders of the Alfa marque that were designed by Pininfarina and first came on the market in 1961. 136 pp, 80 b/w and 12 color photos, English text.

Alfa by Peter Hull. In the Foulis Minimarque Series, a complete history of the marque to 1970. 160 pp, 70 illustrations, English text.

Alfa Romeo 1750 Spider Veloce 1970. Reprint of the works manual in German. A5, 25 pp.

Alfa Romeo 2600 (Berlina/Sprint/Spider) 1964. Reprint of the works manual. A5, 150 pp.

Alfa Romeo 2600 (Berlina/Spider/Sprint). Reprint of the assembly manual for motor, clutch and gearbox. A4, 102 pp.

Alfa Romeo Giulietta Spider/Sprint Veloce/Spider Veloce. Reprint of the assembly manual in German. A4, 265 pp.

Touring Superleggera—Giant among Classic Italian Coachbuilders by Carlo Felice Biancho Anderloni and Angelo Tito Anselmi. This book on the Italian coachbuilding firm of Touring includes many Alfa cars. 252 pp, 600 b/w photos and 8 color plates, English text.

Style Auto 10. Alfa Romeo Giulia Spider Pininfarina. English text.

Alfa Club Journal. This monthly magazine is published by the Classic Alfa Romeo Car Club of Germany.

Quadrifoglio. This quarterly magazine for Alfa Romeo devotees is addressed both to fans of newer Alfa Romeos and admirers of classic Alfas.

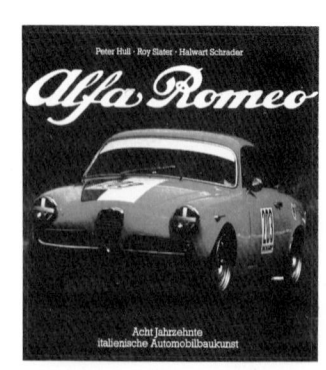

Alfa Romeo Clubs

a Classic Club e.V.
gen Kummer,
erbruchstrasse 31
657 Haan 1
st Germany

aclub e.V.
. Box
531 Guldental
st Germany

a Romeo Club Freiburg e.V.
nd Tritschler, Hurstweg 35
800 Freiburg
st Germany

**b klassischer Alfa-Romeo-
rzeuge e.V.**
assic Alfa Romeo Car Club)
tere Lichtenplatzer Strasse 83
600 Wuppertal 2 (Barmen)
st Germany

Club Alfa Romeo 2600
F. Laufenberg,
Wiedenbrücker Strasse 17
D 4830 Gütersloh
West Germany

Alfa Romeo Model Club
Jürgen Prüfert, Akazienhof 9
D 4100 Duisburg 1
West Germany

Club Alfa Romeo Classico
E. Warnotte, Hinterwisstrasse 3
CH 8123 Ebmatingen
Switzerland

Alfa Romeo Club
P.O. Box 131
CH 3770 Zweisimmen
Switzerland

Registro Alfa Romeo Italiano
c/o Alfa Romeo SpA
I 20020 Arese
Italy

Alfa Romeo Owners' Club UK
Alan Taylor, 37 Amerland Road
London SW 18
England

2000/2600 Register UK
Roger Monk, 14-16 King Street
Leicester LE1
England

Club Alfa Romeo Bezitters
Marijn Jansen, Dussekstraat 113
NL 5011 AH Tilburg
The Netherlands

Miniatuur Alfa Romeo Club
Gijs Jordans, Rozenstraat 13
NL 4613 AH Bergen-op-Zoom
The Netherlands

Alfa Romeo Owner's Club USA
Don Bruno, 501 Irving Avenue
Hillside, Illinois 60162
USA

Alfa Romeo 2500 Club USA
Malcolm Harris, Suite 3210, 1111
Third Avenue
Seattle, Washington 98101
USA

Alfa Romeo Club of Canada
P.O. Box 62, Station Q
Toronto, Ontario M4T 2L7
Canada

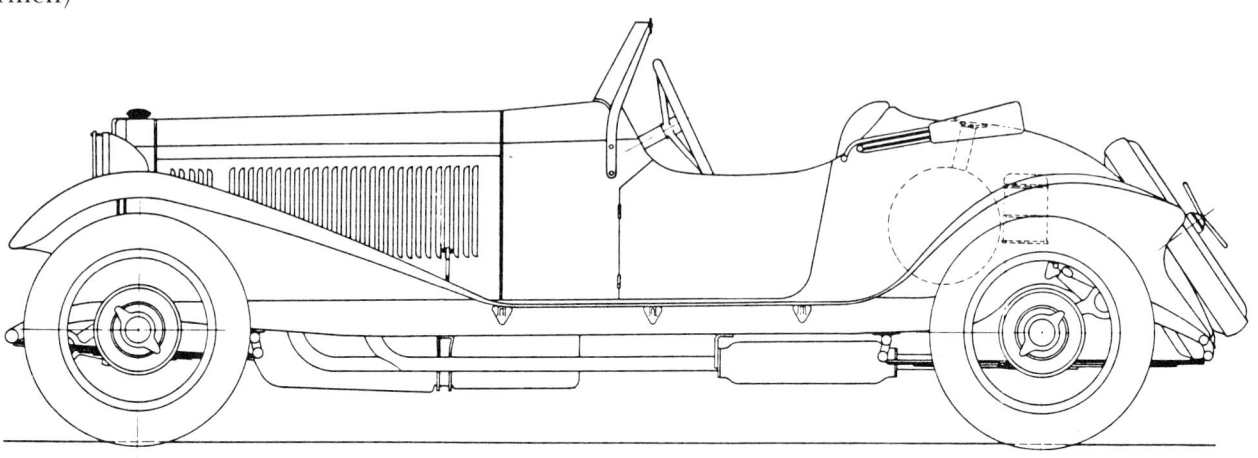